Greater Love Hath No Man

Greater Love Hath No Man

A Series of Lenten Sermons

by

Martin Walker

and

Theophil H. Schroedel

19  47

Concordia Publishing House - Saint Louis

Printed in the United States of America

Foreword

There is no time of the Church Year so conducive to soul winning as the Season of Lent. During this period people seem inclined to be more solemn, more contemplative, more receptive to the deeper things of life.

To help the Lenten preacher to meet this missionary opportunity adequately, we are again publishing a new book of Lenten sermons in the hope that they will be a source of stimulation and inspiration in the preparation of the Lenten preaching program.

THE PUBLISHERS

Table of Contents

Christ For Us and In Us

by Martin Walker

Old Testament Types of Christ

by Theophil H. Schroedel

Christ For Us and In Us

The Courage of Christ

He steadfastly set His face to go to Jerusalem.—Luke 9:51.

The redemption of sin-lost humanity is the great subject of the Bible. There is no grander theme for contemplation to which the mind of man can address itself. St. Peter tells us that God's plan for the salvation of a sin-lost world is a mystery which even the angels desire to look into. In that plan they with their spiritual and heavenly vision behold an amalgam of God's wisdom and power, justice and mercy. With wonderment they behold this combination of God's glorious attributes. If that plan can be of such profound interest to God's angels, who, being sinless, have no part in that redemption, how much more must this divine plan for our salvation challenge our most devout contemplation!

Jesus Christ, in whom alone is our salvation, very properly holds the central place in all our preaching the year around. In the Lenten season we are particularly reminded of the price of our redemption when we meditate upon the Passion of our Lord. Not the other characters who had a part in the story of Christ's Passion, not some peculiar facts or features of that story, but Jesus Christ Himself must ever remain in the center and receive the chief attention. Furthermore, the main emphasis must always be on *what He did for us:* as in His holy life, so also in His bitter suffering and His sacrificial death. "*For us*—for us men and for our salvation"—that is the keynote that must constantly be struck.

Yet there is another fact that must also receive proper emphasis. What Christ did *for us* must now produce something *in us*. His work of redemption is finished. He proclaimed this fact from the Cross. He bids His messengers to go out with His invitation: "Come, for all things are now ready." And the believer's response is:

Nothing in my hand I bring,
Simply to Thy Cross I cling.

Blessed be God, our redemption is complete! But the application of that redemption in our present and future salvation is a continuing process. Our salvation, that is, our *deliverance*, is not only from the curse of the Law and the wrath of God to come, but also from the *present* dominion or rule of sin and Satan. Zacharias, speaking prophetically of this salvation, declares it was God's purpose "that we being *delivered* out of the hand of our enemies might *serve* Him without fear in *holiness* and *righteousness* before Him *all the days of our life*." To the Galatians St. Paul brings a message of grace and peace from Jesus Christ, "who gave Himself for our sins, that He might *deliver* us from this *present* evil world, according to the will of God and our Father." This will of God, stated in other terms of Scripture, means that our justification, which is immediate and complete, must issue in our sanctification, which is a continuing process in this life, finding its completion in life eternal.

This same truth is also set forth in the sacred Scriptures in the following manner. The divine image in which God created man was lost through sin. On the basis of Christ's redemption the Holy Spirit restores this divine image in the believer. This work of restoration remains unfinished in this life. Nevertheless, it is the expressed will of God that we all be "conformed to the image of His Son." Accordingly, we who really hope to be with Christ and like Christ in heaven must strive to become more and more like Christ here on earth.

It is to this last stated fact that we desire to give especial attention in this sermon series. After seeking duly to emphasize what our blessed Redeemer has done *for us,* we aim properly to set forth what He by His Spirit strives to produce *in us.* In this whole series we desire ever to keep in mind that Jesus our *Savior* is also our *Pattern,* as St. Peter so clearly sets forth: "For even hereunto were ye [we] called; because Christ also suffered for us, leaving us an example, that we should follow His steps."

In the first sermon of this series we contemplate

The Courage of Christ

I. For us *II. In us*

I

The Evangelists blanket with silence the youth and early manhood of Jesus in Nazareth. What He said and did we are not told. We do know that He remained sinless. To live a life of moral purity in the midst of sinners must have constantly called for a display of spiritual courage. Certain it is that throughout His public ministry Jesus did display moral heroism. After a brief period of popularity He met increasingly with opposition and persecution. Yet He never showed any signs of fear or weakness. Cowardice was unknown to Him, except as He saw it in others. Behold Him, singlehanded driving the money changers out of the Temple! What moral courage! Read the eighth chapter of St. John, and note how boldly Jesus spoke the most unpleasant truths: "Ye seek to kill Me. . . . Ye are of your father, the devil. . . . If I should say I know Him (the Father) not, I shall be a liar like unto you." When the Pharisees informed Him that King Herod was seeking to kill Him, He replied undauntedly: "Go ye and tell that fox!" Who can read that twenty-third chapter of St. Matthew and not be filled with admiration of the moral heroism of Jesus Christ, standing before His powerful enemies, the proud and much-admired Pharisees, exposing their pretense and hypocrisy, crying one "Woe unto you!" after another, foretelling the wrath of a holy God.

Studded with such displays of courage, His public ministry is a lustrous record. But it is in His Passion that our Savior gave the finest evidence of that spiritual heroism which was so essential an ingredient of His character. In a few simple words Luke gives us an insight into that courageous heart: "He steadfastly set His face to go to Jerusalem." He knew all that was awaiting Him. As He told His disciples of His forthcoming rejection, suffering, and crucifixion, they became timid and fearful. They sought to dissuade Him. "Be it far from Thee, Lord!" exclaimed Peter. Uninfluenced by the fear of His disciples, undeterred by the hatred of His enemies, Jesus steadfastly turned His steps toward Jerusalem. Sublime courage!

"Be strong and of good courage!" Such was the exhortation given by God through Moses to Joshua. Christ, the real Joshua, or Deliverer, needed far greater courage. In His human enemies He saw Satan. Priest and rulers as conspirators and Judas as traitor were but agents of the Prince of Darkness, whose hour had come. Yet, Jesus left the Upper Room in the night of His betrayal with the Great Hallelujah on His lips and walked steadfastly into Gethsemane. There His real humanity manifested itself when He "began to be sore amazed and to be very heavy." Nevertheless, He calmly and bravely went to meet His captors, inquiring fearlessly: "Whom seek ye?" While His disciples forsook Him and fled, He courageously placed Himself into the hands of His enemies, knowing full well that the agony of the Cross was awaiting Him on the morrow.

Very properly do we ask: How was such sublime heroism possible? The answer is: It was begotten of divine love. This love to sin-lost humanity brought Him down from heaven. This love carried Him through all His earthly career; it caused Him to place Himself under the Law and to fulfill it in our stead; it moved Him to take upon Himself our sins and to carry our sorrows; it made Him writhe in Gethsemane under the burden of the world's guilt; it nailed Him to the accursed tree on Calvary, to atone for all the sins of all mankind.

In particular did He by His love-begotten courage *atone for the sins of cowardice.* What an awful record this one sin has made in the history of the world! Through the centuries public officials have, like Pilate, committed crimes in the name of political or public expedience, seeking in vain to wash their hands in innocence. How often have Christ's disciples failed Him because of cowardice! How often have you and I, like Peter, denied Him by silence or betrayed His cause by our moral cowardice! O Jesus! How hast Thou suffered because of our sins! We bless Thee, O Christ, for Thy redeeming love, for Thy heaven-born courage, for all Thy divine virtues!

II

"Let this mind be in you which was also in Christ Jesus." In his Letter to the Philippians, St. Paul applies this exhortation specifically to the virtue of humility. But the exhortation applies with equal force to all the other virtues that characterized the life and the Passion of our Lord. Thus the same

Apostle writes to the Corinthians: "Be ye followers [imitators, R. V.] of me, even as I also am of Christ." According to that divine principle we are not merely to admire the courage displayed by Jesus Christ in His life, more particularly in His Passion, but we are to cherish the desire that a similar courage be begotten in us who bear His name.

Such courage was found in the Apostles of Jesus Christ. Once they had been timid and fearful. In base cowardice Peter denied His Master. All other disciples forsook Him and fled. Even after His resurrection they assembled behind barred doors and locked windows for fear of the Jews. Now read Peter's Pentecostal sermon, in Acts, chapter two. Bear in mind that Peter preached not at some distance from Jerusalem, but in that very city, before the very priests and rulers and people who had delivered Jesus to Pilate to be crucified. To them he says: "God hath made that same Jesus, whom ye have crucified, both Lord and Christ." How account for that change in this man Peter? He had received the Holy Ghost; in other words, he had been filled with the Spirit of Christ. Thus also Christ's courage had been begotten in him. That becomes even more clear as we study the fourth chapter in the Book of Acts. Peter and John had miraculously healed the lame man at the gate of the Temple. Arrested, cast into prison overnight, they on the morrow are on trial before the priests, rulers, and elders. Fearlessly these Apostles proclaim the resurrection of Christ, whom these men had crucified, and boldly they declare that salvation is only in His name. And now we read (v. 14): "When they (these priests and rulers) saw the *boldness* of Peter and John . . . they took knowledge of them that they had been *with Jesus.*" Over against such moral heroism these minions of the devil felt rather helpless. So, after threatening the Apostles, they let them go with the command no more to preach the name of Christ. And what was the final response of Peter and John? "We cannot but speak the things which we have seen and heard." A little later the company of believers in Jerusalem is praying for these men: "Lord, grant unto Thy servants that with all boldness they may speak Thy Word." Some years later the Christian congregation at Jerusalem sends men to Antioch whom they describe as "men that have hazarded their lives for the name of our Lord Jesus Christ." To a large extent the Book of Acts is the record of Christ's courage working in the hearts of His believing disciples.

Look at St. Paul, the Apostle born out of due time. What a career of labor and devotion and sacrifice! Consider the obstacles he had to overcome, the opposition and persecution he had to endure. Read the catalog of his sufferings in Second Corinthians, chapter eleven. Nothing but the courage of Christ could have carried him through it all. And finally, like His Master, he, too, "set his face steadfastly toward Jerusalem." His courageous spirit is expressed in his farewell to the elders of the church at Ephesus: "Behold, I go bound in the spirit unto Jerusalem, not knowing the things that shall befall me there, save that the Holy Ghost witnesseth in every city, saying that bonds and afflictions abide me. But none of these things move me, neither count I my life dear unto myself, so that I might finish my course with joy, and the ministry, which I have received of the Lord Jesus, to testify the Gospel of the grace of God." With the courage of Christ in his heart this great man finished his ministry in the prison at Rome; and sustained by that heaven-born courage, he laid his head on the executioner's block.

Similar courage was displayed by Stephen, the first Christian martyr, and a host of confessors who followed in his train. Without such courage the cause of Christianity would have failed. As it was, "the blood of the martyrs became the seed of the Church."

Such courage, begotten by the indwelling Spirit of Christ, was displayed by Luther and other Reformers, who at the risk of their lives defied the entrenched powers of the Papacy. The moral heroism displayed at Worms by the Monk of Wittenberg was but the courage of Christ in his heart. In the period immediately before and after the Reformation there were thousands of men and women who, having found the pearl of great price in Jesus Christ, "counted not their lives dear," but suffered martyrdom rather than renounce the truth as it is in Christ Jesus. Similar courage was exhibited by the founders and early builders of the Lutheran Church in North America. They defied ecclesiastical authorities in Europe; they forsook all for Christ; they underwent extreme physical hardships; and they had the courage of their convictions in standing aloof from unionistic practices and all forms of error. Often misunderstood and reviled, they courageously confessed the truth as revealed in the sacred Scriptures.

Thus the blessings of Christ's redemption, together with all the treasures of grace in the Gospel and the Sacraments, have been transmitted to us by the fidelity and the courage of the men and women of God through nineteen centuries. What now? Shall Christ not look for similar courage in us?

Now as ever it takes courage to confess Christ before men. It takes courage to proclaim divinely revealed truth without any compromise with error. It takes courage to live a godly life in an ungodly world. It takes courage for Christian youth to say No to the blandishments and allurements of a lustful world. It takes courage for Christian men and women to refuse to unite with social and quasi-religious organizations that have a ritual from which the name of our blessed Savior is barred. Yes, it takes courage day by day to be honest in business over against dishonest competition; to be industrious at work when others loaf and rebuke you for conscientious performance of duty. It takes courage to stand apart from the mob and to walk singly in the narrow way of righteousness. And, finally, it takes courage to bear the burdens, the disappointments, the griefs of life, patiently and uncomplainingly. In short, it requires courage to take up Christ's cross and follow Him. Yet, it is just that which He rightly expects of those whom He has bought with a price and to whom He has promised His Spirit.

How, then, shall we secure such courage? The answer is quite simple. Courage is but the expression of a strong faith. Now, faith is begotten in us by the Word; and it is nourished by the Word and the Sacrament. The more frequently and the more devoutly we hear and read the Gospel of Christ, the more will our faith in Him be strengthened, and the more will His courage be generated within us. Moreover, as Jesus Himself constantly communed with His Father in prayer in order to receive courage from on high, even so must we commune diligently with Christ in prayer so that we may "be strengthened with might by His Spirit in the inner man." More particularly will we gain courage from Christ by a devout contemplation of His Passion, of all that He endured for us men and for our salvation. Yes, as we observe the many instances of Christ's high courage, it is as though we heard Him calling to us: "Come, follow Me, follow My example!" "For even hereunto were we called; because Christ also suffered for us, leaving us an example, that we should follow His steps."

Finally, courage, like all other Christian virtues, must be developed in practice. As every shirking of duty leaves us morally weaker, so every performance of duty makes us morally stronger. To overcome moral cowardice, we must practice the Christian virtue of courage.

Look about you in this disordered and distracted world. What is needed? More men of brilliance? More women of smartness? No, and a thousand times, No! What this troubled world needs is men of spiritual vision and moral courage, men who fear God and dare to do His will. And what is needed also in the Church of Jesus Christ is more men who, "in-filled" with the Spirit of Christ, will fearlessly proclaim the truth and live the truth—men who will courageously fight the battles of our Lord against error, unbelief, and every form of wrong. "Watch ye, stand fast in the faith, quit you like men, be strong!"

Stand up! Stand up for Jesus!
The trumpet call obey;
Forth to the mighty conflict
In this His glorious day!
Ye that are men, now serve Him
Against unnumbered foes;
Let courage rise with danger,
And strength to strength oppose. Amen.

The Submission of Christ

And He went a little farther and fell on His face and prayed, saying, O My Father, if it be possible, let this cup pass from Me; nevertheless not as I will, but as Thou wilt. . . . He went away again the second time and prayed, saying, O My Father, if this cup may not pass away from Me except I drink it, Thy will be done. . . . And He left them and went away again and prayed the third time, saying the same words.—MATTHEW 26:39, 42, 44.

THE whole earthly life of Jesus Christ was one of submission to His Father's will.

When we speak of this submission, we are at once confronted by the deep mystery that lies in the Bible doctrine of the blessed Trinity. Within that Trinity there could be no conflict of wills. Jesus, as a member of that Trinity, had in eternity helped to plan the divine counsel regarding the redemption of a sin-lost world. However, on assuming our human nature, the eternal Son of God voluntarily subjected Himself to the will of His Father. His whole state of humiliation was one of subjection and obedience. In the 40th Psalm, Christ is heard to speak prophetically: "Lo, I come. In the volume of the Book it is written of Me, I delight to do Thy will, O My God; yea, Thy Law is within My heart." In a discussion with the Jews, Jesus declared: "I came down from heaven, not to do Mine own will, but the will of Him that sent Me" (John 6:38). Both at the end of His private life and at the close of His public ministry, marked respectively by His Baptism and His transfiguration, Jesus received the commendation of His Father: "This is My beloved Son, in whom I am well pleased." The divinely inspired testimony of the Apostle is: "He humbled Himself and became obedient unto death."

However, we may not disregard that other declaration of Holy Writ: "He was in all points tempted as we are, yet without sin." To us this must ever remain a deep mystery. Jesus was tempted, truly tempted. He was tempted to disregard the Father's will. He was tempted to go the easy way, to please Himself, to escape shame and suffering and death. Had He yielded to this temptation, His lifework would have been ruined. He would have become a sinner, and we would have remained lost and condemned sinners.

But, blessed be God, Jesus overcame the Tempter, not only immediately after His Baptism, but all through His life and labors. He overcame the Tempter when the conflict grew hottest, in the Garden of Gethsemane. We shall never be able to understand the terrific struggle that went on in the soul of Jesus. Satan was making his final onslaught to wreck the work of Christ and to prevent the world's redemption. But Jesus conquered. He conquered in agonizing prayer. He conquered by submission to the Father's will.

We contemplate

The Submission of Christ

I. For us *II. In us*

I

In the last year of His public ministry Jesus became more and more "a man of sorrows and acquainted with grief." The hatred of His enemies steadily increased. "He was despised and rejected of men." All this did not surprise Jesus. He had foreseen it all. Calmly He spoke with His disciples regarding the schemes of His enemies, always referring them to the Scriptures of the Old Testament. Clearly He foretold His great Passion. With sublime courage He steadfastly set His face to go to Jerusalem. In the night of betrayal He resolutely wended His steps to Gethsemane.

There, under the unspeakable burden of the world's sin and guilt, this sinless Son of God was writhing in indescribable agony of soul. He was tasting the bitter cup of the divine wrath over man's transgressions of God's holy Law. Yes, He, the Substitute, the Sin-Bearer, was suffering the curse of the broken Law. He, the God-Man, with His divine foreknowledge, saw clearly all that was awaiting Him on the morrow: shame, mockery, rejection, crucifixion. Anguish seized upon His soul. His sweat was like drops of blood. His strength was gone. He was utterly exhausted.

In deepest anguish He cried out: "O My Father, if it be possible, let this cup pass from Me." He felt that He could go no farther; He must have relief. In His humiliation He had become so intensely human as to shrink back from the awful torture that was awaiting Him. It seems as though the divine counsel for our redemption, the plan which He Himself had helped to devise, was hidden from His view or beclouded in His mind. The mystery is too deep for us. How intensely Jesus suffered in His soul, how truly He dreaded all that He was yet to endure, is clearly shown by the fact that after brief intervals He begged the Father a second and a third time to take this cup of suffering and woe from Him. Referring, no doubt, to this scene, the writer of the Letter to the Hebrews declares that our Savior "offered up prayers and supplications with strong crying and tears unto Him that was able to save Him from death."

Yet, in all that earnest prayer, there was no sinful desire to escape duty. There was not the slightest murmur or complaint. On the contrary, the spirit of filial submission to the Father's will undergirded that whole petition. Note the condition that Jesus wove into His petition, even the first time: *"If it be possible."* Jesus is not at variance with the Father's will to save sin-lost humanity. He has neither lost sight of the need of man's redemption, nor has He lost interest in the sinner's welfare. "If it be possible"—those very words were an expression of submission. According to the detailed account in St. Matthew, Jesus appears to have regained some inner composure and to have become more resigned to the Father's will by the time He uttered the petition the second and third times. For note the change in wording. He now prays: "O My Father, *if this cup may NOT pass away from Me except I drink it, Thy will be done."*

"Not as I will, but as Thou wilt." "Thy will be done." There was consternation in hell and joy in heaven when Jesus spoke those words. For in them He expressed fully and finally His unreserved submission to the Father's will. In such perfect obedience He fulfilled all righteousness. Thus He, the second Adam, made good the disobedience of the first Adam. "As by one man's disobedience many were made sinners, so by the obedience of One shall many be made righteous." By His willing submission to the Father's will our Savior made full atonement for our self-will, for our refusal to submit unreservedly and constantly to the divine will. As we recognize and lament our sins of disobedience and insubordination, we find that the Father in great mercy has already accounted to us the perfect obedience and submission of His Son. Thus we are redeemed, forgiven. Yet, we are redeemed not only from the guilt and the punishment of these sins, but also from the dominion of Satan, who prompts these sins within us. Hence our sorrow over these sins and our faith in Jesus Christ must constantly evidence themselves in the sincere endeavor to practice in our own lives the obedience and submission manifested by our Savior.

II

All that Christ did *for us* must now become a fact *within us*. "For even hereunto were ye called: because Christ also suffered for us, leaving us an example, that ye should follow His steps."

True, we have in the Biblical records other examples of submission to the divine will. We hear High Priest Eli saying in great distress of soul: "It is the Lord; let Him do what seemeth Him good." We hear Job, after suffering the loss of all, saying: "The Lord gave, the Lord hath taken away; blessed be the name of the Lord." Abraham became the father of believers by constantly submitting to the inscrutable will of God. The Virgin Mary, perplexed and mystified, humbly submits to the divine plan: "Behold, the handmaiden of the Lord; be it unto me according to Thy Word."

But Jesus is the perfect Example of obedience and submission. We are absolutely safe in always keeping our eye on Him as the true Pattern of every form of godliness. More than that. He becomes *the new motivation* in the life of the believer. By faith His Spirit dwells within us. With the great Apostle each of us must be able to say that in some degree "Christ liveth in me."

By precept and by example Jesus taught His disciples to pray: *"Thy will be done."* In His holy Word God reveals His will to us. It is our simple duty to know and then to do God's will. There will be times when it will be fairly easy for us to do God's will. We are able to recognize the wisdom and the goodness of God in that will. We realize it is for our welfare. We learn to say that His commandments are not grievous. According to the inward man we learn to delight in the Law of the Lord. But more often we find the will of God hard. For we are still in the flesh. Our old Adam asserts himself. Satan stirs up revolt within us. Then we look upon Jesus, our Savior and our Pattern. Remembering the price of our redemption, and hearing again His prayer in the garden, we learn anew to pray with Him: "Not as I will, but as Thou wilt." Flesh and blood are conquered; the Spirit triumphs; and we delight to do God's will. We enjoy the benediction of our Savior: "Whosoever shall do the will of God, the same is My brother and My sister and mother."

Not always can we see the sun of God's grace shining brightly upon us. Into most Christian lives there come hours and days, and to many there come months and years, when the sunshine of divine favor is obscured by the clouds of adversity. We may lose employment and income; sustain reverses and losses in business; meet with many perplexing and trying situations; have one disappointment after another. We wonder whether God is with us. We are tempted to doubt and to complain. Or the Lord visits our home with a great sorrow. Father or Mother may be taken from us; without their presence the home is broken. A sister or a brother, whose life was a part of our very own, is removed from the family circle. A child on whom we affectionately placed our hopes for the future is laid low in death. Can it be that these things come from God? Our faith is sorely tried. Or we ourselves are laid on a bed of sickness. We suffer pains of body; perhaps also agony of mind. We pray for relief, but it comes not; we beg for restoration of health and strength, but it is not granted. Again we are tempted to murmur and complain. Then we go to dark Gethsemane. We note our Savior's agony; we hear the cry of His grief-stricken heart. But we also hear His words of submission: "Not as I will, but as Thou wilt." We hear His words of resignation: "Thy will be done." We learn of Jesus Christ to pray. His Spirit comes upon us. Like our beloved Master, we resign ourselves to our Father's will, knowing that it is wise and just, full of love and grace. And in submission we find peace and inward strength.

Yet one more thought. At the outset I said that the whole life of Jesus was one of submission. Thus He was prepared for the hardest and final test in Gethsemane. In the Letter to the Hebrews we are told that the Captain of our salvation was made perfect through sufferings. And again: "Though He were a Son, yet learned He obedience by the things which He suffered; and being made perfect, He became the Author of eternal salvation unto all them that obey Him." Likewise we. Not in an hour of crisis, not by some sudden effort, can we acquire this attitude of submission to our heavenly Father's will. But we must discipline our souls in the routine of life, in our daily conduct, to say: "Not my will, but Thy will be done." To remind us of our duty daily to submit our will to the will of our heavenly Father, Jesus teaches us daily to pray: "Thy will be done." Now, if we not only speak those words, but sincerely pray them day by day; if furthermore we will act accordingly and truly submit our will to God's will in all things, then we shall develop an attitude of submission

The Patience of Christ

Jesus held His peace.—MATTHEW 26:33.
We exhort you, brethren . . . be patient toward all men.—
1 THESSALONIANS 5:14.

The Lord direct your hearts into the love of God and into the patience of Christ.—2 THESSALONIANS 3:5 (R. V.).

NO ONE who is at all familiar with the life of Christ would doubt for a moment that He was a man of patience. Yet, strangely enough, the virtue of patience is not directly attributed to Christ in any of the four Gospels. Nevertheless, as we study these accounts, we find many instances of Christ's patience with His disciples, with the multitudes, and with His enemies. And as we read the Epistles, we find that the Apostles had been deeply impressed by the patience and forbearance of their beloved Master. This patience, as we shall see, was a twin virtue with His submission to the Father's will. In a measure it was in patience that His submission found expression. Because Jesus was so submissive to His Father's will, He was enabled to be so patient in the many trying circumstances of His earthly career and finally also in His great Passion.

In this Lenten meditation we shall dwell on

THE PATIENCE OF JESUS

I. For us *II. In us*

I

As we read the account of the last Passover meal in the

Upper Room in Jerusalem, we are impressed with the patience which Jesus exercised with His disciples. They were unwilling to render each other the service of footwashing; they continued to ask foolish questions; they were slow to comprehend what He was saying; and to the last they retained human and false ideas regarding the Kingdom. Patiently Jesus continued to instruct and guide them. Patiently He bore with the traitorous disciple. In the Garden of Gethsemane even the most trusted disciples failed Jesus. He so longed for their companionship, for a word of cheer or sympathy. But they were dull, unresponsive, sleepy. Yet patiently and kindly He said: "Sleep on now, and take your rest." When Judas gave Him that treacherous kiss, Jesus did not smite him to the ground, but patiently withheld all punishment. Patiently He bore the manifold indignities heaped upon Him by His captors.

Behold Jesus in the court of the priests. What holy indignation must have filled His breast over against the pretenses of the high priest, the false testimony of the perjured witnesses, the hypocrisy that ran through all the proceedings! Yet, in divine patience, He refrained from uttering words in which He might have unmasked their hypocrisy and announced God's wrath upon them. "He held His peace." How patiently He bore with the Temple police who smote Him and buffeted Him and even spit in His holy face! Behold our Savior in the court of Pilate. He is unjustly scourged, but He utters no protest. Soldiers and others mock Him, they have cruel sport with Him: place a reed in His hand as imitation of a royal scepter and press a crown of thorns upon His sensitive brow, causing excruciating pain; they cover His lacerated back with an imitation royal purple robe and mockingly bow their knees before Him. Patiently Jesus puts up with it all. He makes no request for protection or for justice. "Behold the Man!" "He kept His peace."

Behold Jesus bearing His Cross. Patiently He drags the load without asking relief. He succumbs under the burden, and then Simon is compelled to carry the Cross the last part of the way. Patiently He endured the shame and the pain of the crucifixion and the taunts and jeers of the priests and people who reviled Him and challenged Him to come down from the Cross. Oh, what patience! what fortitude! what restraint! what divine forbearance!

Why all this patience? Why this marvelous and sustained patience in the garden, in the courts of Jews and Romans, on the Via Dolorosa, and on the Cross? *"For us! for us!"* that is the simple and meaningful answer. For us He endured all pain and shame. For us He withheld all exercise of the divine power latent within Him. For us He suffered patiently to atone for our sins of impatience, for our many displays of sudden anger, of impulsive and hurtful wrath. The patience of Jesus was the patience of the Lamb of God, taking away the sins of the world.

Lamb of God, pure and holy,
  Who on the Cross didst suffer,
Ever patient and lowly,
  Thyself to scorn didst offer.
All sins Thou borest for us,
  Else had despair reigned o'er us:
Have mercy on us, O Jesus!

II

This patience of Jesus must now be reproduced in us who bear His name. To the Christians in Thessalonica St. Paul wrote: "The Lord direct your hearts into the love of God and into the *patience of Christ.*" This Apostolic prayer was heard.

The Thessalonian Christians, persecuted by the Jews, remained steadfast in the faith and suffered in patience. The Spirit of Christ imparted this patience to them. With gratitude to God St. Paul could write to them: "We remember without ceasing your work of faith and labor of love and patience of hope in our Lord Jesus Christ." Writing to his young co-workers Timothy and Titus, Paul inculcates *patience* as one of the outstanding virtues to be found in those who would be workers in the Kingdom. Defending his own apostolate over against the false teachers in Corinth, St. Paul points to his record during eighteen months of labor in their midst: "Approving ourselves as ministers of God in much *patience*." And again: "Truly the signs of an Apostle were wrought among you in all *patience*."

Even so we need to take to heart the Apostolic injunction: "Let us run with *patience* the race that is set before us, *looking unto Jesus*, the Author and Finisher of our faith." Only as we look to Jesus and keep our eyes fixed on His example of patience, we can learn to be patient and steadfast in our individual lives as well as in our corporate work in the Kingdom. He labored for us and suffered for us, leaving us an example, that we should follow in His steps.

This patience of our Lord Jesus Christ must be reproduced in us also in our relationships with our fellow men. How great is the need of patience here! How many there be that try our patience! How easily we are led into displays of impatience! How often may we have unintentionally bruised a heart that we love by a show of impatience! No doubt there is a difference here, also among regenerate men, according to one's natural disposition. A person with a phlegmatic temperament will not be so readily aroused to impatience as another with an impulsive disposition. Even so, whatever be our natural temperament, we all need to learn patience in our dealings with our fellow men, especially with those who in one way or another offend us. Christ expects this of us; and He, our Savior, has also set His pattern before us that we may be His imitators.

Those early Christians in Thessalonica, hated and persecuted, must have found it hard to remain patient. To them Paul wrote: "We exhort you, brethren . . . be patient toward all men." By their patience they proved themselves genuine disciples of Jesus Christ. May we be given grace to be patient toward all, forgiving and forbearing, even as our heavenly Father for Christ's sake is patient with us.

"The God of patience and consolation grant you to be likeminded one toward another according to Christ Jesus." Amen.

The Silence of Christ

The high priest stood up in the midst and asked Jesus, saying, Answerest Thou nothing? What is it which these witness against Thee? But He held His peace and answered nothing. —MARK 14:60-61a.

The chief priests accused Him of many things, but He answered nothing. And Pilate asked Him again, saying, Answerest Thou nothing? Behold how many things they witness against Thee. But Jesus yet answered nothing, so that Pilate marveled.—MARK 15:3-5.

Then he [Herod] questioned with Him in many words; but He answered him nothing.—LUKE 23:9.

NO ONE can read the Gospel account of Christ's Passion without being impressed by His dignified and majestic silence.

This silence of Jesus was neither the silence of ignorance nor of fear. Particularly in the last year of His public ministry, Jesus fearlessly faced His enemies and boldly told them very unpleasant truths about themselves. Quoting from the Old Testament Scriptures, He uncovered their ignorance. When they spoke insincerely and pretentiously, He unmasked their hypocrisy. When they sought to take Him in His talk, He turned the tables on them. By His powerful words of divine wisdom He silenced His gainsayers.

But when the time for His suffering came, the time for speaking had ended. One of the distinguishing marks of the suffering Servant of God, the Messiah of Israel, as portrayed in the 53d chapter of Isaiah, was His *silence.* "He was oppressed, and He was afflicted, yet He opened not His mouth. He is brought as a lamb to the slaughter, and as a sheep before her shearers is dumb, so He openeth not His mouth." That impressive silence was part of the price of our redemption. In such silence our suffering Savior also has left us an example that we are to pattern after.

The Silence of Jesus

I. For us *II. In us*

I

The silence of our Savior during His Passion becomes all the more impressive when set in contrast to His readiness of speech during His public ministry. For three years He mingled with His countrymen in Galilee and Judea, and also visited Samaria, everywhere preaching the Gospel of the Kingdom. On the Sabbath and on weekdays, from morning till night, to the multitudes, to small groups, and to individuals, He taught the will of His Father and revealed Himself as the Messiah of Israel, the Redeemer of all mankind. At times He preached for hours to large assemblies; at other times He spoke at length with an individual, as with Nicodemus the Pharisee and the Samaritan woman of Sychar. He spoke gently to the weak, sympathetically to the sorrowing, and sternly to the wicked. With fiery eloquence and divine indignation He denounced the hypocritical Pharisees and the unbelieving Sadducees. The agents of His enemies were compelled to report: "Never a man spake as this Man." And before Caiaphas, Jesus could testify: "I spake openly to the world . . . in secret have I said nothing."

Even in His Passion, Jesus withheld not the word of truth and of love. Both in the court of the Jews and in the court of the Romans He replied to the essential questions put to Him authoritatively by Caiaphas and Pilate. He refused not to testify. He, the Savior of sinners, sought even to reach the heart and conscience of the pagan governor. But over against the false accusations of the Jewish rulers; over against the cries of the misguided mob; over against the indignities of Jewish Temple police and Roman soldiers; over against the hypocrisy of Caiaphas and the injustice of Pilate—over against all these Jesus remained eloquently silent. Surely, such silence deeply impressed His enemies.

Likewise Jesus remained silent in the intensest agonies of soul and body. Carrying His heavy Cross, He complained not and asked not for relief. While the malefactors reviled and cursed, the great Sufferer silently prayed. Thus He consciously fulfilled the prophecy in Isaiah, as St. Peter tells us: "When He was reviled, He reviled not again; when He suffered, He threatened not; but committed Himself to Him that judgeth righteously."

What, now, was *the meaning and purpose of this silence?* We need not speculate. The Scriptures make it clear. The silent Sufferer was the Lamb of God, bearing and taking away the sin of the world. By His silence He indicated His *willingness* to suffer shame and reproach, injustice and injury, pain and torment. Yea, more. By His silence He made atonement for the sins of men, particularly the sins of the tongue. Only the recording angels know how many and how manifold are the sins committed by the children of Adam with their tongues. There are the sins against the Second Commandment: the thoughtless use and the downright misuse of God's holy name. Think of the countless curses on the street and the innumerable false oaths in the courts! Think of the misuse of the name of holy God in designedly false and deceptive teaching, in imitations of Christianity, in false religious practices, in hypocritical prayers! Think of the sins against the Fourth Commandment: in words of disrespect and disobedience to fathers and mothers, in words that wound their hearts and even shorten their lives; in words of disrespect to lawful rulers or in harsh and unjust criticisms of others in authority. Think of the sins against the Fifth Commandment: in words of sinful anger and wrath, of threat and violence, words that lead to bloodshed and even war. Think of the sins against the Sixth Commandment: in words of impurity, of suggestive and smutty stories, words that often lead to outright fornication and adultery. Think of the sins against the Eighth Commandment: in words that express an offhand and uncharitable judgment of the neighbor's motives; in words that misinterpret his actions; in words that slander and defame his character, that rob him of his good name! Oh, how many, how great, how vile are the sins of the tongue! What strife, what havoc have they wrought in the world! Writes St. James: "Behold, how great a matter a little fire kindleth! And the tongue is a fire, a world of iniquity."

Are *we* free of these sins? Remember, they were very educated and refined people, these Pharisees and Sadducees, who slandered and defamed Jesus of Nazareth; very religious people who falsely accused this Man and plotted His death; they were synogog-trained and Temple-going citizens of Jerusalem that shouted: "Crucify Him!" They were punctilious observers of religious customs who, standing beneath the Cross, mocked the Crucified! Bear in mind, it was to Christians, or at least professing Christians, that St. James wrote: "Out of the same mouth proceedeth blessing and cursing. My brethren, these things ought not so to be." Ah, yes, we, too, have sinned with our tongues, sinned more frequently than we know, sinned more grievously than we are aware, done more harm than we realize.

Oh, many a shaft at random sent
Finds mark the archer little meant!
And many a word at random spoken
May soothe, or wound, a heart that's broken! (Scott.)

For these our sins Jesus suffered; for these sins He made atonement in the deep silence of His great Passion.

For this silence we bless Thee, dear Jesus. We pray Thee, impart unto us Thy Spirit of patience—forbearance—silence.

II

The Savior, who by His silence atoned for our sins of the tongue, also left us an example that we are to pattern after. His silence is to be reproduced in us who bear His name. From Him we are to learn how to keep silent, when such is the will of our heavenly Father.

There is, says Solomon, "a time to keep silence and a time to speak" (Eccl. 3:7). There is a time to speak for the honor of God and the building of our beloved Savior's Church on earth. Gladly we should proclaim the truth as revealed to us in the Bible. Willingly we should witness for Christ before friend or foe. According to our station and our opportunity we should instruct, guide, warn, rebuke, with all long-suffering and kindness. Yet, there is a time to keep silent. We do not owe an answer to all the malicious criticisms of God and the Bible. We need not reply to every wicked slur upon Christ and Christianity. A Christlike silence will in many instances be more effective than voluble argumentation. The same holds true when the integrity of our own character is questioned, when our good name is involved. It is perfectly proper to defend ourselves against false accusations; we may even have to go to court to protect the honor of our good name. Then there are other times when it is wiser, more Christlike, to suffer in silence; better not to dignify every attack with a reply. Sometimes no answer is the best answer.

Especially must we guard our tongue when we are vexed, when tempted to make an angry reply. "Let every man be swift to hear, slow to speak, slow to wrath; for the wrath of man worketh not the righteousness of God," writes St. James. And Solomon declares: "Whoso keepeth his mouth and his tongue keepeth his soul from troubles" (Prov. 21:23).

In general, we who are Christ's disciples must cultivate more of the quiet, peaceable, patient spirit that dwelt in Him. "Learn of Me," He said, "for I am meek and lowly in heart." By a Christlike silence we may reveal to others something of the beauty and the grace of Him who was and remains both our Savior and our Pattern.

God, give us grace to do this. Amen.

The Compassion of Christ

When He saw the multitudes, He was moved with compassion on them.—Matthew 9:36.

And when He was come near, He beheld the city and wept over it.—Luke 19:41.

Bear ye one another's burdens, and so fulfill the law of Christ. —Galatians 6:2.

The Lord of heaven and earth in His infinite wisdom chose to reveal Himself in His true nature to the people of Israel as to no other nation. By nature all men have some knowledge of God. But this limited knowledge has been corrupted by sin. The most enlightened of heathen nations conceived of their gods as endowed with wisdom and power, but not with absolute holiness and justice. To their false gods they attributed vengeance and vindictiveness, also vacillation and weakness, even moral turpitude; but no pity and no mercy. The true God, however, revealed Himself to His chosen people not only as a God of infinite wisdom and power, of holiness and justice, but also of truth and grace. Thus, when the Lord on Mount Sinai gave to Moses the second set of two tables of stone with the Ten Commandments, He proclaimed: "The Lord, the Lord God, merciful and gracious, long-suffering, and abundant in goodness and truth, keeping mercy for thousands, forgiving iniquity and transgression and sin."

Through the centuries the Lord sent His prophets to Israel. The messages of these prophets were largely a condemnation of sin and an announcement of God's wrath over the transgressors. Yet all these prophets were commissioned to announce to the penitent that the Lord is "merciful and gracious,"eager to forgive and to restore. In particular did these prophets point to the coming Messiah, who would "redeem Israel from all his iniquities."

Yet even Israel had an inadequate conception of the mercy of God. "The Law was given by Moses; but grace and truth came by Jesus Christ." When the Word was made flesh, when the Son of God became man and dwelt among men, then the greatest truth ever revealed to a sin-lost world became apparent: *"God is Love!"* This transcendent truth Jesus taught by word of mouth and by His whole redemptive work, both in His holy life and in His sacrificial death. In Jesus of Nazareth the compassion of God was personalized. When the Apostle declares: "We beheld His glory," he emphasizes that this God-Man was "full of grace and truth."

We meditate upon

The Compassion of Jesus

I. For us *II. In us*

I

Isaiah, the pre-eminently evangelical Prophet, represents the coming Messiah as declaring: "The Lord hath anointed Me to preach good tidings unto the meek; He hath sent Me to bind up the brokenhearted, to proclaim liberty to the captives, and the opening of the prison to them that are bound; to proclaim the acceptable year of the Lord and the day of vengeance of our God; to comfort all that mourn." When Jesus preached His first sermon in Nazareth, He applied these words to Himself. Yes, in Jesus, the eternal Son of the

Father, divine Compassion came down from heaven to earth.

What was it that moved the Son of God to leave His heavenly glory, to live and labor, to suffer and die on this sin-cursed earth? It was, in a word, *compassion*. We are more familiar with the word sympathy—a term not used in our older English Bible translations. Sympathy, or compassion, means fellowship in suffering. It means, entering so deeply into the misery of another as to feel it with him and even to be willing to suffer in order to bring relief to the other. Such is divine sympathy, or compassion. It is infinite pity bestowed on the miserable; it is undeserved mercy granted to the guilty. It is God suffering for and with men.

Such compassion motivated the whole life of Jesus of Nazareth. This becomes very clear in the record of His public ministry. "He went about doing good." He responded graciously to the cry of the needy, the distressed, the afflicted. He waited not to be called. He went out of His way to seek the sufferer and to grant relief. A typical picture of Christ's merciful ministry is drawn for us by St. Matthew in the following words: "When the even was come, they brought unto Him many that were possessed with devils; and He cast out the spirits with His Word and healed all that were sick, that it might be fulfilled which was spoken by Esaias the Prophet, saying, Himself took our infirmities and bare our sicknesses." We can take time tonight to look at only a few of the Gospel accounts that tell of this compassion of Jesus. In the story of the feeding of the five thousand we read: "Jesus called His disciples unto Him and said, I have *compassion* on the multitude, because they continue with Me now three days and have nothing to eat, and I will not send them away fasting, lest they faint in the way." Though primarily interested in men's souls, the compassionate Savior was not unmindful of the needs of their bodies. It is so today. With reference to the physically afflicted we read: "Jesus, moved with *compassion,* put forth His hand and touched him (the leper) and saith unto him: I will, be thou clean." Again, with reference to the two blind men of Jericho, we read: "So Jesus had *compassion* on them and touched their eyes, and immediately their eyes received sight, and they followed Him" (Matt. 20:34). Jesus felt a deep compassion for those bereft of loved ones through death. Thus we read that when He came to Nain and saw the widowed mother following the bier of her only son, "He had *compassion* on her and said: Weep not," and forthwith restored the son to his mother. And later at the grave of His friend Lazarus the compassionate Jesus wept — wept in sympathy not only with Mary and Martha, but with all humanity—wept because sin and death had gained such cruel power over man.

Yes, beneath all human misery the divine eye of Jesus saw sin. He fed and healed men's bodies in order to heal and nourish their sin-sick souls. He was, first and foremost, compassionate with the children of Adam in their *spiritual distress.* Thus we read: "When He saw the multitudes, He was moved with *compassion* on them, because they fainted and were scattered abroad, as sheep having no shepherd" (Matt. 9:36). Behold the God-Man, near the close of His work on earth, riding on a beast of burden down the western slope of the Mount of Olives, overlooking Jerusalem. Luke tells us: "He beheld the city and wept over it, saying: If thou hadst known, even thou, at least in this thy day, the things which belong unto thy peace! But now they are hid from thine eyes." And St. Matthew reports the mournful cry that issued from the compassionate heart of our Redeemer two days later: "O Jerusalem, Jerusalem, thou that killest the prophets and stonest them which are sent unto thee, how often would I have gathered thy children together, even as a hen gathereth her chickens under her wings, and ye would not!"

Even in His great Passion our Savior's thoughts were not of Himself, but of others. When the women of Jerusalem wept over Him as He dragged His heavy Cross toward Golgotha, He said to them: "Weep not for Me, but for yourselves and your children." His divine eye foresaw the impending doom of Jerusalem and the awful suffering of its inhabitants; and His compassionate heart bled for them. In Gethsemane, Jesus had compassion on Malchus, whose ear, in misguided defense of His Master, Peter had cut off. Jesus replaced the ear. At the same time the Master felt concern and compassion for His helpless disciples. With a show of divine authority He said to the Jewish and Roman police: "If ye seek Me, let these (disciples) go their way." On the Cross He had compassion on His tormentors and prayed for them. Likewise He had compassion on the penitent thief, at once responded to His petition, and assured Him of immediate entrance into Paradise. He had compassion with His mother, suffering under the Cross, and tenderly said to her: "Woman, behold thy son," thus providing for her by turning her over to the beloved disciple.

In all this compassion Jesus was expressing His Savior-love to sin-lost humanity. By these acts of compassion He was atoning for man's sins of selfishness, of lovelessness, of coldness and hardness of heart, and of downright cruelty. What an awful mess the world is in today because of these sins! And in these sins of the world we, too, have had our part. How often have we been guilty of a lack of pity and mercy! How often have we "passed by on the other side"! How often have we failed to be sympathetic and compassionate! Lord, have mercy upon us!

Not only was Jesus compassionate while on earth. He is still compassionate, as our High Priest and Advocate at the right hand of the Father. How gracious the assurance in the fourth chapter of Hebrews: "We have not an High Priest which cannot be touched with the feeling of our infirmities; but was in all points tempted like as we are, yet without sin. Let us therefore come boldly unto the throne of grace, that we may obtain mercy and find grace to help in time of need." How gracious the invitation which Jesus still extends to us in His Gospel: "Come unto Me, all ye that labor and are heavy laden, and I will give you rest . . . rest unto your souls."

II

Like our blessed Lord and Savior we, too, must be compassionate. His Spirit of compassion must dwell in our hearts. "Let this mind be in you which was also in Christ Jesus."

Even in the Old Covenant the God of Mercy required His people to be merciful. "Thus speaketh the Lord of Hosts, saying, Execute true judgment, and show mercy and compassions every man to his brother" (Zach. 7:9). And in Micah 6:8 we find the oft-quoted passage: "He hath showed thee, O man, what is good; and what doth the Lord require of thee but to do justly and *to love mercy* and to walk humbly with thy God?" In the story of the man fallen among the thieves Jesus rebuked the priest and the Levite for coldly passing by on the other side and held up the Good Samaritan, who "had compassion on him," as an example to be followed. "Go, and do thou likewise."

Now this compassion that God requires of us is something entirely different from that maudlin sentiment that causes some women to bring flowers and bonbons to willful criminals; or that moves people to shed tears when in the theater they behold scenes of imaginary suffering, and then to go forth and remain indifferent and cold toward real suffering. This compassion that the God of Mercy seeks in His children is more than mere human sympathy. It is a divine affection. And the pattern that Jesus has left us is our constant invitation to *be* like Him and to *go* and *do* likewise. "Let this mind be in you which was also in Christ Jesus."

Like our divine Master, we, His late-born disciples, must show compassion with our fellow men in the manifold troubles of life. "Bear ye one another's burdens, and so fulfill the law of Christ." For such sharing of burdens there will be no lack of opportunity. About us are the lonesome souls and the brokenhearted, the aged and infirm, the neglected children, the sick and invalid, the homes darkened by the death of a loved one. How great the need for "the cup of cold water," the hand of human helpfulness, the word of divine sympathy and comfort!

Someone near you is struggling alone
  Over life's desert sand;
Faith, hope, and courage together are gone—
  Reach him a helping hand.
Turn on his darkness a beam of your light,
  Soothe his discouragement, heal his affright,
  Lovingly help him to stand.

Then there are those about us who have grieved and harmed us. These are to become the objects not of our hatred, but rather of our pity. Remember Christ's Parable of the Unmerciful Servant. "O thou wicked servant, I forgave thee all that debt, because thou desiredst me. Shouldest not thou also have had compassion on thy fellow servant, even as I had pity on thee?" Awful is the lot of those who receive mercy and render none! Likewise there are the weak and erring brethren in the Christian community for whom we as true Christians, as "Christ's men," must have compassionate regard. Thus writes the Apostle: "We, then, that are strong ought to bear the infirmities of the weak and not to please ourselves. . . . For even Christ pleased not Himself" (Rom. 15:1, 3).

What a picture of destitution and desolation the war-ravaged countries of the world present today! Misery on a hitherto unknown scale! Ruined homes, famished bodies, broken spirits! Men, women, and children, by the hundreds of thousands in Europe and in Asia, starving physically for lack of food and starving spiritually for want of the Bread of Life and the Water of Life! What would our compassionate Savior do were He now on earth? He *is* now on earth in the person of His disciples. Does He acknowledge us as such? Then remember: He has no feet but our feet to run His errands of mercy; no hands but our hands to extend His help; no hearts but our hearts to pour out compassion to suffering humanity. He is counting on us. Dare we fail Him?

If, like our beloved Master, we compassionately combine spiritual and physical relief also to those who once were our enemies, we shall prove ourselves children of our Father which is in heaven, and at the same time we shall be making the best possible contribution to the restoration of peace in a war-weary world. God bless our efforts for Jesus' sake. Amen.

The Love of Christ

Jesus . . . having loved His own which were in the world, He loved them unto the end.—JOHN 13:1.

A new commandment I give unto you, That ye love one another; as I have loved you, that ye also love one another. By this shall all men know that ye are My disciples, if ye have love one to another.—JOHN 13:34-35.

Herein is love, not that we loved God, but that He loved us and sent His Son to be the Propitiation for our sins. Beloved, if God so loved us, we ought also to love one another.—1 JOHN 4:10-11.

"GOD is love." In all of the world's religious literature there is expressed no sublimer thought than that. And this truth, that God is love, is found only in the Bible. The most cultured pagans who wrote religious philosophies no more discovered this truth than did the most benighted heathen. "God is love." Alas, that this divinely revealed truth should be so much misunderstood and misapplied! "God is love." This does not mean that there is any moral weakness in God, that He compromises with error or winks at wrong. Quite the contrary. This is the glory of God's love that without doing violence to holiness, justice, and truth, it could find expression in mercy. God's love is so transcendently beautiful and adorable because it is bestowed upon the loveless, the needy, the unworthy. God's love takes on the form of pity on the worthless, the vile, the rebellious. And such are we all by nature,

"God so loved the world that He gave His only-begotten Son, that whosoever believeth in Him should not perish, but have everlasting life." Into those few, marvelous words Jesus compressed the truth about God's love: its depth, its expression, its universality, its purpose, its achievement, and the manner in which that love is to be appropriated. There is a lifetime of study in these words as well as a daily supply of comfort for every believer. What needs to be emphasized again and again is that the love of God is only in Christ and through Christ; that apart from the only-begotten Son there is no love, no mercy, no salvation and life.

This love of God in Christ is so wonderful that, as St. Paul writes, it surpasses knowledge. There is in this love a length and breadth, a depth and height, that we cannot comprehend with our finite minds. Nevertheless, we who by the Holy Spirit have been moved to accept in simple faith the blessings of this divine love should never cease to meditate devoutly upon the record of this love of God in Christ, as given in the Gospel. Then shall we enter more deeply into a grateful appreciation of this wondrous love, and its saving and transforming power will become more manifest in our lives.

In our Lenten devotions we have thus far meditated on "The Courage of Christ," "The Submission of Christ," "The Patience of Christ," "The Silence of Christ," and "The Compassion of Christ." Now, the love of Christ, which we shall contemplate this evening, is not something apart from the foregoing virtues in Christ. Rather, it is the fountain whence flowed all these other virtues. We look tonight into the very heart of Jesus and pray that our hearts may be warmed by His love and filled with His love.

We contemplate

The Love of Christ

I. For us *II. In us*

I

"When Jesus knew that His hour was come that He should depart out of this world unto the Father, having loved His own which were in the world, He loved them unto the end." With these touching words John, the disciple of love, introduces his report of the Passover Feast and Christ's farewell talks in the Upper Room in Jerusalem, in the night of His betrayal. "He loved them to the end." Here is the *constancy* of divine love. Again and again the disciples had proved themselves weak, vacillating, undependable, faithless. Yet Jesus "loved them to the end." Who but Jesus would have shown them such persevering patience and kindness?—Are not we like these first disciples? just as unworthy as they? just as undependable? Have we not, like them, again and again sinned against His love and forbearance? Yet He loves *us* to the *end.* "Love divine, all love excelling!" The persistency of that love is our only comfort and hope.

Think of the *greatness of Christ's love.* "As my Father hath loved Me, so have I loved you" (John 15:9). Who can measure the greatness of the Father's love to His Son? It is an ocean of love without bottom. Who are we, what goodness is there in us, that Jesus should at all love us? And now to think that He, the Holy One, should love us unworthy sinners even as the Father has loved Him from eternity! It is too wonderful! The contemplation of such love must first humble us deeply and then uplift us mightily. In the greatness of that love the Son has "washed us from our sins in His own blood and has made us kings and priests unto God and His Father" (Rev.

1:5-6). Not until we are with Him in heaven will we fully understand what that means.

Consider the *depth* of that love. "Greater love hath no man than this, that a man lay down his life for his friends," said Jesus to His disciples in that night of betrayal. And then He went forth and laid down His life for His enemies—which included all mankind. Here is the inspired comment in Romans, chapter five, on that marvelous love: "Scarcely for a righteous man will one die; yet, peradventure, for a good man some would even dare to die. But God commendeth His love toward us in that, while we were yet *sinners* (v. 10: "when we were *enemies*"), Christ died for us." We need not look at the criminal element in the world to gain an idea of the depths to which the sacrificial love of Christ stooped down; we need only look into our own hearts and at our own records. As we do so, we shall fall down adoringly at the foot of Christ's Cross and join the Apostle John in this confession: "Herein is love, not that we loved God, but that He loved us and sent His Son to be the Propitiation for our sins" (I John 4:10). "Love divine, all love excelling!" Truly,

> The love of Jesus, what it is,
> None but His loved ones know.

Wondering at that love, admiring its beauty, and trusting it for our redemption, you and I may say humbly, joyfully, gratefully: "He loved *me* and gave Himself for *me*" (Gal. 2:20).

"For us"—this is the Gospel, the good news. For us He left His throne and came into the world.

> Nothing brought Him from above,
> Nothing but redeeming love.

For us He lived a life of perfect obedience to the Father's will. For us He labored; for us He suffered misunderstanding, hatred, loneliness, rejection of men. For us He went into Gethsemane, enduring agony of soul in conflict with Satan. For us He bore the Cross, weighted by the sin of the world, even our own sin. For us He walked step by step from Nazareth to Golgotha, courageously, submissively, patiently, silently, compassionately, lovingly.

By such love the Son of God redeemed us from the curse of the Law, which divine Justice would have to pronounce on us who have failed to keep the law of love. How loveless is our conduct over against our neighbor, whom we should love as ourselves! Worse still, how sadly have we failed to love with all our heart, with all our soul, and with all our mind Him from whom all blessings flow, our God, to whom we owe all that we are and have, who despite our unworthiness loves us with an everlasting love! Blessed be the loving Christ, who by the sacrifice of Himself has made propitiation for our sins and reconciled us unto God!

II

In those profound heart talks which the Master had with His disciples in the Upper Room He spoke not only about the greatness of His love to them, but also of *the love which He expected from them.* True to the very nature of His love, its utter selflessness, He did give them commandment to love one another. However, He knew full well that the Old Testament Law, which required love, had not produced it and that likewise a mere commandment from Him requiring love from them would be no more effective. He therefore first reminds them of the greatness of His love to them: "As the Father hath loved Me, so have I loved you"; and then He pleads with them: "Continue ye in My love." He was confident that if His disciples would abide in His love, then they would in return love not only Him, but also one another. So it came to pass. The disciple of love later reports: "We love Him because He first loved us."—Even so shall it be with us late-born disciples. In the measure in which we abide in Christ's love shall we love Him and one another.

Now note how Jesus spoke to those who would abide in His love: "A new commandment I give unto you, That ye love one another; as I have loved you, that ye also love one another." The commandment to love our neighbor as ourselves was indeed old. But there are two elements in Christ's commandment that differentiate it from the old and that make it a new commandment: first, Christ here specifically inculcates *love among His disciples,* a new, higher, purer type of love among those who have been blessed by the fellowship of His love; secondly, Christ's commandment is new with respect to *the degree of love:* "as I have loved you." Such love among human beings is possible only in the circle of those who have tasted and who continue to taste the sweetness of Christ's love, who experience its cleansing and sanctifying power.—This, then, is His commandment to us: to love one another, to love the brethren and sisters in the household of faith, even as He has loved us. It is a lofty requirement. But the more we drink of the fountain of Christ's love, in His Gospel and Sacrament, the better shall we be enabled to meet that requirement.

Moreover, we observe that Jesus has made this love a *test of discipleship.* "By this shall all men know that ye are My disciples, if ye have love one to another." These disciples and their immediate converts in Jerusalem met this test. Their love to one another was so great that it became sacrificial. Those who had possessions sold them and placed the money in a common treasury for the benefit of the poor. Thus we read: "Neither was there any among them that lacked." Similarly the early Christians among the Gentiles manifested such a high degree of love to each other that the pagans marveled and exclaimed: "See, how they love each other!" Yes, by their love-filled lives these early Christians attracted many of their neighbors to Christ.—Are we doing as well? That becomes a question for each disciple to answer. We all, no doubt, fall far short of the high standard Christ has set for us: "As I have loved you." But to the glory of our Savior be it said that even today there is such a fine spirit of love prevailing *among His true disciples* that the world is still constrained to take note. Even the world of unbelievers must acknowledge that Christianity, with its principle of love, is the only moral power which can change hatred to love, and warfare to peace and good will.

Love to the brethren is thus also *the test of our love to God,* the touchstone of our spiritual life. "He that loveth not His brother whom he hath seen, how can he love God, whom he hath not seen?" (1 John 4:20.) There is much vague profession of love to God; but it fails in its practical test. Professing Christians whose lives are not characterized by love, who show little or no compassion for their needy and suffering brethren, need to heed this Apostolic appeal: "Beloved, if God *so* loved us, we ought also to love one another" (I John 4:11); "Let us not love in word, neither in tongue, but in deed and in truth" (1 John 3:18).

Oh, may the love of Christ, which we have again so richly tasted in this blessed Lenten season, abide in our hearts! May it constrain us to love Him fervently, who gave Himself for us, and also to love sincerely all those for whom He bled and died.

"Be ye therefore followers of God, as dear children; and walk in love, as Christ also hath loved us and hath given Himself for us an offering and a sacrifice to God for a sweet-smelling savor."—Amen.

The Death of Christ

Jesus cried with a loud voice and gave up the ghost.—MARK 15:37.

God commendeth His love toward us in that, while we were yet sinners, Christ died for us.—ROMANS 5:8.

I am crucified with Christ. Nevertheless, I live; yet not I, but Christ liveth in me; and the life which I now live in the flesh I live by the faith of the Son of God, who loved me and gave Himself for me.—GALATIANS 2:20.

ANOTHER Lenten season is drawing to its close. It has been one more season of divine grace, the last, no doubt, for some of us! Again we have beheld the Son of God as the Lamb of God, bearing and taking away the sin of the world—even our own sin.

In our Lenten meditations this year we took particular note of the great virtues which Jesus displayed in His life, especially also in His Passion. We noted how these virtues all were the expression of the divine love that moved the Son of God to come into this sin-cursed world "to seek and to save that which was lost." His courage, His submission, His patience, His silence, His compassion, His comprehensive love—all were elements of His obedience, whereby He fulfilled all righteousness; all were elements in His redemptive work, whereby He made atonement for the transgressions of all men. All these virtues were displayed for us, for our salvation, culminating in His death for us on the Cross,

But we also noted that these divine virtues work something in us. Though there still are many who can "see no beauty nor comeliness" in Christ that they should desire Him as their Savior, we have been so enlightened by the Holy Spirit that we can truly sing and say: "Beautiful Savior! Truly I'd love Thee; truly I'd serve Thee." His virtues have for us a beauty, an attractiveness, a transforming power, so that we desire to be like Him.

I long to be like Jesus, meek, loving, lowly, mild;
I long to be like Jesus, the Father's holy Child.

We shall strive, at least in some degree, to manifest Christ's virtues in our own lives, so that we may be Christians indeed, Christ's men and women, that the world may take note that we have been with Jesus. In so far as we are Christians, we shall sincerely desire to let this mind be in us which was also in Christ Jesus; and we shall endeavor, not only in the Lenten season, but all the year through, to remember the Apostolic admonition: "Hereunto were ye called: because Christ also suffered for us, leaving us an example, that ye should follow His steps."

As we this day stand beneath the Cross, we contemplate

The Death of Christ

I. For us *II. In us*

I

With simple dignity all four Evangelists report the death of the God-Man Jesus on the Cross of Calvary. They do so in almost identical words: "He bowed His head and gave up the ghost." It was *a real death,* a sundering of the ties that bound soul and body together. His death came after He had suffered indescribable agony of soul and torture of body.

Moreover, it was a public death. Jesus did not die in solitude, in some secret chamber, nor yet in the presence of only a friend or two. He died in the sight of many, in the presence of His enemies, as a result of an official sentence of death which was publicly executed. Thus the fact of Christ's death was officially attested. There can be no doubt: Jesus of Nazareth, who claimed to be, and by His life and teaching and miracles proved Himself to be, the Son of God, truly died on the Cross of Calvary.

Withal it was *a voluntary death.* Though betrayed by a disciple, though persecuted by priests and rulers, though condemned to death by an unjust judge, though executed by Roman soldiers, yet Jesus died of His own free will. He repeatedly foretold His early death. To Nicodemus He had said: "As Moses lifted up the serpent in the wilderness, even so must the Son of Man be lifted up." In the last months of His sojourn on earth Jesus frequently spoke to His disciples about His impending rejection and crucifixion. Jesus declared: "I lay down My life. . . . No man taketh it from Me, but I lay it down of Myself. I have power to lay it down, and I have power to take it again." Voluntarily He delivered Himself up to His captors in Gethsemane. And when taunted by the priests, though He had power to come down from the Cross, He *chose* to remain on the Cross, because He had come "to *give* His life a ransom for many."

Yes, this real and voluntary death of Jesus was *a sacrificial death.* Thus it was foretold. "He was wounded for our transgressions, He was bruised for our iniquities. . . . The Lord hath laid on Him the iniquity of us all. . . . Thou shalt make His soul an *offering for sin.* . . . He hath poured out His soul unto death. . . . He bare the sin of many" (Is. 53). Jesus Himself declared: "I am the Good Shepherd; the Good Shepherd giveth His life for the sheep. . . . I lay down My life for the sheep." The inspired Apostles all proclaim the death of Christ as sacrificial and substitutionary for the redemption of sinful humanity. Thus writes St. Paul: "When we were yet without strength, in due time, Christ died for the ungodly. . . . God commendeth His love toward us in that, while we were yet sinners, Christ died for us. . . . Christ died for our sins according to the Scriptures." St. Peter writes: "Christ His own self bare our sins in His own body on the tree. . . . For Christ also hath once suffered for sins, the Just for the unjust, that He might bring us to God, being put to death in the flesh, but quickened by the spirit." And St. John writes: "Hereby perceive we the love of God, because He laid down His life for us."

This sacrificial death was also *a fruitful death.* Jesus neither suffered nor died in vain. Isaiah foretold: "He shall see His seed (that is, His spiritual descendants, the lives He saved by His death). . . . He shall see of the travail of His soul (that is, see the fruit of His Passion) and shall be satisfied." Jesus well knew that His death would bring life to the world. He rejoiced in advance over the fruit of His sacrifice. The note of joy and thanksgiving rings forth in His great high-priestly prayer (John 17). St. Paul declares: "Christ was delivered for our offenses and raised again for our justification (our forgiveness)." Again: "When we were enemies, we were *reconciled* to God by the death of His Son. . . . We also joy in God through our Lord Jesus Christ, by whom we have now received the *Atonement.*" St. John writes: "In this was manifested the love of God toward us, because that God sent His only-begotten Son into the world, that we might live through Him. Herein is love, not that we loved God, but that He loved us and sent His Son to be the Propitiation for our sins."

The theme song of the redeemed in heaven is the praise of the Lamb upon the throne: "Thou wast slain and hast *redeemed* us unto God by Thy blood, out of every kindred, and tongue, and people, and nation; and hast made us unto our God kings and priests."

For us men and for our salvation the Son of God became man. For us, for you and for me, He was born in lowliness at Bethlehem; for us He lived the life of purity in Nazareth; for us He fulfilled all righteousness in His manhood; for us He suffered reproaches and rejection; for us He went into Gethsemane and on to Golgotha; for us He was forsaken of God on the Cross; for us He tasted the extreme bitterness of death. For us, as our Substitute, He suffered the curse of the broken Law of holy God; for us He paid the penalty of our guilt. "By His stripes we are healed."

Oh, may these divine revelations, these wondrous truths, never become commonplace to us! As we tonight look upon the Son of God, laying down His life on the altar of the Cross, may we be smitten with a deep sense of sin, with a painful consciousness that we—not only Jews and Romans, not only the vile criminals of our day—we ourselves by our known and unknown sins have nailed the Son of God to the accursed tree. May we behold the Lamb of God penitently, believingly, gratefully.

Thou hast suffered great affliction
And hast borne it patiently,
Even death by crucifixion,
That Thou might'st atone for me.
Thou didst choose to be tormented
That my doom should be prevented.
Thousand, thousand thanks shall be,
Dearest Jesus, unto Thee.

II

"Let us also go that we may die with Him." Thus spoke Thomas when Jesus declared His intention to go back to Judea, though He knew that the Jews were plotting to kill Him. In Thomas, as in all the disciples, the spirit was willing, but the flesh weak. He was not prepared to die with Jesus. And yet, in a sense that Thomas could not understand until after Pentecost, he *had* to die with Jesus, and actually *did* die, when Jesus died on the Cross. That was true of all the eleven disciples; and that is still true of us late-born disciples, true of all who by the Holy Spirit are through faith brought into fellowship with Christ.

This is true in a twofold sense. We died with Christ because the Father of mercy accounts the death of Christ as the payment of our debt. He regards us as having died when Christ died on the Cross in our stead. That is clear teaching of Scripture. (2 Cor. 5:14.) We died with Christ: that is true also in this sense that as Christ died *for* our sins, so we have died *to* sin, to the world, and to self. That is the Apostolic argumentation in Romans, chapter six, over against those who abuse the doctrine of grace. Let us hear some of this great Apostolic message: "Shall we continue in sin that grace may abound? God forbid! How shall we that are dead to sin live any longer therein? . . . Our old man (our sinful nature) is crucified with Him, that the body of sin might be destroyed, that henceforth we should not serve sin."

Now, when we by the power of Christ's death die unto sin, we are at the same time quickened into a newness of life, as St. Paul teaches in this same passage. "We are buried with Christ by Baptism *into death,* that like as Christ was raised up from the dead by the glory of the Father, even so we also should walk *in newness of life.* . . . Reckon ye also yourselves to be *dead* indeed unto sin, but *alive* unto God through Jesus Christ, our Lord." Similarly St. Peter: "Christ His own self bare our sins in His own body on the tree, that we, being *dead to sins,* should *live* unto righteousness." "If any man be in Christ," by a living faith, "he is a new creature," a new life having been created within him. "Old things," such as the old self-will, love of self and of the world, "are passed away, all things are become new." Spiritual life, the life of faith in Christ, always implies a daily dying to sin and to the world and to self—the old sinful nature. That is the significance of our Baptism: that "the old Adam in us should by daily contrition and repentance be drowned and *die* with all sins and evil lusts and, again, a new man daily come forth and arise, who shall live before God in righteousness and purity forever." This daily dying unto sin, the world, and self is a painful process. "Mortify"—that is, kill off—"therefore your members which are upon the earth" (Col. 3:5); and then follows a whole catalog of sins to which we Christians are daily tempted. But "they that are Christ's have crucified the flesh with the affections and lusts" (Gal. 5:24). In the power of Christ's death and resurrection we, too, through the indwelling of His Spirit, can achieve a great victory. St. Paul could declare: "God forbid that I should glory, save in the Cross of our Lord Jesus Christ, by whom the world is crucified unto me and I unto the world." And so we sing:

Forbid it, Lord, that I should boast
  Save in the death of Christ, my God;
All the vain things that charm me most,
  I sacrifice them to His blood.

Who of us can hear or read this noble confession of St. Paul and not be deeply moved thereby: "I am crucified (mark well, *crucified!*) with Christ. Nevertheless, I live; yet not I, but Christ liveth in me. And the life which I now live in the flesh I live by the faith of the Son of God, who loved me and gave Himself for me" (Gal. 2:20). If in this Lenten season we have devoutly meditated upon the Passion of our Lord as the price of our redemption; if on this Good Friday, with godly sorrow, we look up to the thorn-crowned, bleeding, dying Savior of men, you and I also may say with genuine faith and deep emotion: "He loved *me* and gave Himself for *me.*" Then we shall also pray to be given grace to say: "I am crucified with Christ. Nevertheless . . . Christ liveth in me." "For to me to live is Christ; to die is gain."

Finally, in the power of Christ's death, we, too, may die peacefully and triumphantly. Without Christ we should dread even the temporal death; for to the unsaved soul the first death is but the gateway to the second death, eternal death, the eternal separation from the God of light and truth and love, the everlasting punishment in the fire of hell, prepared for the devil and his angels. But we who through faith in Christ's death have been reconciled to God are saved from the second death and hence need not fear the first death. In the power of Christ's death and resurrection we calmly face death and say with the great Apostle: "O Death, where is thy sting? O Grave, where is thy victory?" As we close our eyes in death, we know ourselves secure in the wounds of Christ, where there is forgiveness, life, and salvation. May the prayer of our childhood be our prayer throughout life and in the hour of our departure:

Old Testament Types of Christ

The Offering of Isaac

And it came to pass after these things that God did tempt Abraham and said unto him: Abraham; and he said: Behold, here I am. And he said: Take now thy son, thine only son Isaac, whom thou lovest, and get thee into the land of Moriah, and offer him there for a burnt offering upon one of the mountains which I will tell thee of. And Abraham rose up early in the morning and saddled his ass and took two of his young men with him and Isaac his son and clave the wood for the burnt offering and rose up and went unto the place of which God had told him. Then on the third day Abraham lifted up his eyes and saw the place afar off.

And Abraham built an altar there and laid the wood in order and bound Isaac his son and laid him on the altar upon the wood. And Abraham stretched forth his hand and took the knife to slay his son. And the angel of the Lord called unto him out of heaven and said: Abraham, Abraham! And he said: Here am I. And he said: Lay not thine hand upon the lad, neither do thou anything unto him; for now I know that thou fearest God, seeing thou hast not withheld thy son, thine only son from Me.—GENESIS 22:1-4, 9-12.

ONCE more by the mercy of God we come to a new series of Lenten services. It is well that we set aside a special evening every week to follow our Lord on the way to Calvary and to think of the great facts of our Christian religion. I thank God that you have interrupted the routine of your daily life and torn yourself away from the things that occupy so much of your attention and have come to the house of God to spend a quiet evening hour with your fellow Christians.

The purpose of our being here is expressed in the opening stanza of the Lenten hymn, so appropriate for an Ash Wednesday service, "Jesus, I will ponder now on Thy holy Passion." Thus we are beginning another pilgrimage to Calvary; but this year our approach will be different from the usual one. We shall see our Lord in the light of the Old Testament. There are a great many incidents, facts, and objects in the Old Testament which have direct reference to Christ and His redemptive work. We speak of them as types, and they find their fulfillment in the life and death of our Lord.

The first in the series is the offering of Isaac. There are two persons in this story, father and son, Abraham and Isaac. Our attention is directed first to the father. Abraham was one of the great and good men of the Old Testament, and the Bible tells us of many incidents in his life. As we read the story of his life, we find a phrase which occurs again and again: "And there Abraham built an altar unto the Lord." That was characteristic of this man of God. There have been in our times men whom later generations will be able to follow on the pages of history by the trail of blood that they left. But Abraham may be followed through the Promised Land by his altars, which fact is an evidence of his trust and faith in God. But of all the altars that he ever built there was none more important in his life than the one referred to here. For this is the altar on which he was to sacrifice his own son, to give into death the joy and pride of his life.

I need not repeat to you the details of the story. You know it well. Suffice it to say that he had waited years and years, until his old age, for the birth of his child. This was to be no ordinary son. Abraham had been given the promise that through him all the nations were to be blessed. It was a great test of faith to believe in these promises. Finally the fulfillment came. The son was born. Can you imagine how much he loved him? Not only because he was long expected and flesh of his own flesh, but because he was to be the channel through which God was to reveal Himself.

But then came the great blow. One evening, as perhaps he was looking up to the stars, which to him had become a symbol of the faithfulness of God and of the hopes of the future, God said to him: "Take Isaac, whom thou lovest, and go to Mount Moriah and offer him as a sacrifice to Me." What a request that was! How it must have cut Abraham to the quick! What agonies he must have suffered that night! Perhaps you fathers and mothers can feel like Abraham in a little way when you think of the time you said good-bye to your son, when he took his last leave to go overseas. But the Bible does not tell us what went on in the father's heart. It says nothing about the struggle between the love he bore his only son and his trust in the faithfulness of God. When the morning came, Abraham set out to do the bidding of the Lord.

For three days father and son walked together. The destination was Mount Moriah, later a part of Jerusalem. The summit of that mountain is a great rock. I had the privilege of seeing it while in Jerusalem. Now there is a beautiful building, one of the most beautiful in the world, erected over it, and as we stand gazing upon that rock we can faintly imagine the feelings in Abraham's heart as he put one stone upon another. But he did it with a marvelous faith that God would be able to raise his son from the dead. Nowhere else in Scripture is there anything like it. Abraham is the great hero of faith. It is in his footsteps that others have followed, like Job, the patient sufferer, who in the depths of his misery cried out: "Though He slay me, yet will I trust in Him." It is here where we might well ask ourselves: How strong is our faith? Do we come through every test with an unwavering trust in God? When everything goes well, it may be easy to believe in the justice and goodness of God, but what if God should ever ask us to go to Mount Moriah, if He should take away from us the things we love, to which our hearts are attached, if He should demand of us, as He did of Abraham, to give up a beloved member of our family? That, however, is not the subject upon which I should like to enter tonight.

We have something more important to consider, for this is a touching human picture of the divine sacrifice God made when He placed His Son on the path that led to the altar of the Cross. It is an Old Testament type of the fact so beautifully expressed by John: "God so loved the world that He gave His only-begotten Son." The real test of love is the sacrifice that someone is willing to make. That is true of us, and it is true of God, and God went the very limit. He gave the best that He had. He placed His Son on the path that led to the death on the Cross. Now, it is quite surprising how many parallels we are able to find between the sacrifice of Isaac and the sacrifice of Christ. Isaac was the father's only son. He was long expected. He came by a miracle. He had done nothing worthy of death. He carried his own wood. He was silent and spoke only once, and to the father he was practically dead for three days. You see, wherever we turn, the offering of Isaac is a type of the sacrifice of Christ.

We are told that Catherine, the wife of Martin Luther, was very much perturbed about this story. She could not understand why God should ask Abraham to slay his own son. But Luther answered: "If that is true, then how can we understand that God should give His own Son into death?"

As we look out upon the world today, lately bathed in

blood and even now suffering from fear, hatred, and cruelty, there are two great facts that stand out above all others. The first is one everyone can see, that no one dare deny. The other one we see only when we are enlightened by the Spirit of God. The first is the sinfulness of man, his pride, his lust for power, his capacity to hate and destroy, to allow himself to become a tool of the devil. The other, which we can see nowhere except in the Word of God and cannot understand unless we are enlightened by the Spirit of God, is that God had compassion on this world of sin and determined to save it. When we join these two facts, then we get the true meaning of Lent and of Calvary, for the Cross means that God is reaching down from heaven into a world perishing in its sins. He who was betrayed by His own disciples, rejected by His own people, condemned to the Cross by the pagan powers of the world, is none other than God's great gift to the world, to me and to every believer. Therefore, if there is any conviction that I must have on this Ash Wednesday, it is this that over against all the sin and faithlessness of man, even over against my own shortcomings, wrongs, and frailties I am able to proclaim that God loves me, that He has made a great sacrifice for me, that He has given me a great gift and assures me that this brief broken and mortal life can have immortal meaning.

It is here where we can look into the great Father-heart of God. God knew that there was only one way by which the world could be saved, and that was by the sacrifice of His own Son. And He did it gladly, out of love for you and me. This means our atonement. It means that Christ took our place, that He paid the penalty which we could not pay. That is the essence of Christianity, and there only remains for us that we accept it, believe and put our trust in it. Then we have passed from death into life.

Joseph and His Brethren

And Joseph said unto his brethren: Come near to me, I pray you. And they came near. And he said: I am Joseph, your brother, whom ye sold into Egypt. Now therefore be not grieved nor angry with yourselves that ye sold me hither; for God did send me before you to preserve life.—GENESIS 45:4-5.

WHICH do you think are the world's greatest stories? Answers to this question may differ widely, but there are two that I have in mind tonight which I know rank among the very greatest. Both of them have to do with boys who were lost. One of these stories is found in the New Testament. It is one of the parables of Jesus. The name by which it is known is "The Prodigal Son." It is one of the most beautiful and touching stories ever written. Here is a boy who is lost, truly lost, lost to shame, to filial love, to gratitude and purity. But here also is a loving father who longs for his son's return, and when the son does repent, he opens his arms to receive him again.

But there is another story equally great. We find it in the Old Testament. It also has to do with a boy who was lost. It tells of Joseph, and we find in it the great emotions that take hold of human hearts, the buoyancy of youth, the destructive fire of lust, loyalty to home ideals, sorrow and joy. Above all do we see the marvelous hand of God, who rules in the lives of His enemies and of His children and overrules the evil of men so that it may be turned into good for those who love and serve Him. It is a remarkable story also from another standpoint, for Joseph is a type of Christ, and many of his experiences prefigure incidents in the Passion of our Lord. That, too, is the reason why we are especially interested in the story of Joseph tonight, for it is to commemorate our Lord's Passion that we are gathered here in this evening hour.

There isn't time to enter into the details of the entire story. We can merely touch on some of the high points. One such high point is indicated in these words: "I am Joseph, your brother, whom ye sold into Egypt." Joseph was one of the twelve sons of Jacob. He was his father's favorite son, and that led to difficulties. It is never good for parents to favor one child over against another, or for the father to favor one, and the mother another. We can see the evil results here, for Joseph was hated by his brothers, who at first decided to kill him and then sold him into slavery. In the land of Egypt he came into the house of an official by the name of Potiphar. Because he was a young man of great ability and winsome personality, he advanced to the chief post in his master's house.

But with responsibility there also came temptation, and the temptress in this case was the wife of his master. It was a temptation such as can come to any man or woman, and if he had yielded, he would have done himself and others untold harm. That's the kind of temptation our young men and women away from home are subject to, and when we think of that, there ought to be the fervent prayer in our hearts that they come out of temptation as Joseph did and remember the word of Scripture that their bodies are the temple of the Holy Spirit.

Speaking of temptations, do you remember the Gospel of last Sunday which told how our Lord was led into the wilderness to be tempted by the devil? We see how Satan tried one device after another. He offered Him what the hearts of men have always desired—personal comfort, wealth, and power. But Jesus was not overcome, for He had an effective means of defense, the Word of God. That is what we ought to keep in mind when we are tempted, for temptations will come because "the devil as a roaring lion walketh about seeking whom he may devour." Whenever temptation comes, there is virtue in flight; but if we cannot flee, we must know that we can win in the struggle if we remain close to God and His Word. That, too, was the path that Joseph took when he said: "How, then, can I do this great wickedness and sin against God?"

There isn't time to dwell on the results of his refusal to sin. Suffice it to say that after many other experiences Joseph was made prime minister of the realm. His life's story reads like a fairy tale. It is the story of the slave who became prime minister. Here too, as so often is the case in the dealings of God with man, truth is stranger than fiction. The climax of his life comes when his own brothers arrive in Egypt. He recognizes them, but they do not recognize him. He tests them and, having found them to be changed men, reveals himself to them and forgives them all their wrong.

Now, it is right here, as well as in other experiences, that Joseph is a type of Christ. It is quite surprising how many parallels we see between Joseph and Christ, especially Christ in His Passion. Joseph was hated by his brothers. So Jesus "came into His own, and His own received Him not." The brothers planned to kill Joseph, just as the chief priests laid their wicked plans to kill the Son of God. Joseph was sold into slavery; so Judas sold his Master for thirty pieces of silver. Joseph was tempted, and so Jesus was tempted in the Garden of Gethsemane. Joseph was accused of great wrongs and placed into prison. So Jesus was accused unjustly of having threatened to destroy the Temple and of being a rebel against the Roman government. Yet Joseph shows utmost patience, and in like manner Jesus was like a lamb led to the slaughter.

The story of Joseph is one of injustice and hardship, but it proves that God can bring good out of evil. "Ye thought evil against me, but God meant it unto good," Joseph said to those who had wronged him so grievously. Thereby he expressed a great and wonderful truth. Centuries later, Paul put it into these words: "All things work together for good to them that love God." Through the wickedness of his brothers Joseph became a slave in Egypt. But there it was that God raised him to power so that in the years of famine he might be the savior of all the people of Egypt and of his own father and brothers as well. In like manner through the death of Christ, brought about by wicked men, God was able to accomplish a great redemption.

Especially beautiful and touching is the incident mentioned in our text. Joseph is confronting his brethren. They had caused him terrible agony. What would you and I have done under like circumstances? It is so human to retaliate, to pay back in the same coin. But Joseph seems to have heard the voice of Christ: "Love your enemies, bless them that curse you, do good to them that hate you, and pray for them which despitefully use you and persecute you." There are instances where people waited for years until they could get their revenge. But do you believe that they were happy while they brooded over their hurt, waiting for the time when they could return injury for injury? No, indeed. They were far from happy. They were miserable. "Revenge is sweet" is a popular proverb, but it is not true. It is a lie. Revenge is never sweet. It always puts hell into one's heart. But what a blessed thing it is to forgive, to return good for evil! How it adds joy to one's life and brings heaven down to earth!

But it is especially when we are standing at the foot of the Cross that we see so clearly the blessed truth of forgiveness. There is no anger or resentment in the heart of Him who is hanging upon the central Cross. There is no unwillingness to obey. Every thought of Himself is swallowed up in His great love. There is a cry for mercy, but it is not for Himself, but rather for His enemies. "Father, forgive them, for they know not what they do." Nowhere else do we so clearly see the reality of sin, for it was for the sins of the world, for yours and mine, that He was crucified. Nowhere else is there impressed upon us so deeply the blessed truth of forgiveness.

What is it that men can do about their sins? Some treat them lightly, some try to forget them, others regret their wrongs deeply and are even driven to despair, but men cannot forgive them. That can be done only through the blood of Christ. Thus by looking into the soul of Christ through this window of His first word from the Cross we are brought face to face with the heart of the Bible. Forgiveness is one of the great words of the Bible. It stands beside other great words as repentance, faith, hope, and love. The fact is that forgiveness is the very center of our Christian religion. If God had not been willing to forgive, Christ would not have come down to earth. If God had not been willing to forgive, we would not now be His children and the heirs of heaven.

Now, while forgiveness is the essence of Christianity, and while to forgive the sins of men is the great mission of Christ, for us to forgive those who hurt us is the heart of practical Christianity. For did not the Lord teach us to pray: "Forgive us our trespasses as we forgive those who trespass against us"? But is not God demanding something exceedingly difficult?

The Passover Lamb

Speak ye unto all the congregation of Israel, saying: In the tenth day of this month they shall take to them every man a lamb, according to the house of their fathers, a lamb for an house. Your lamb shall be without blemish, a male of the first year . . . and the whole assembly of the congregation of Israel shall kill it in the evening. And they shall take of the blood and strike it on the two side posts and on the upper door post of the houses wherein they shall eat it. And they shall eat the flesh in that night, roast with fire, and unleavened bread, and with bitter herbs.

For I will pass through the land of Egypt this night and will smite all the firstborn in the land of Egypt. . . . And the blood shall be to you for a token upon the houses where ye are; and when I see the blood, I will pass over you, and the plague shall not be upon you to destroy you, when I smite the land of Egypt.—Exodus 12:3, 5, 8, 12, 13.

The years of war, still vivid in our memory, were years when people were on the march. Not only was there a great shift of population from the rural districts to the cities and from one end of the country to the other, but great masses of people in Europe and Asia were driven from one territory to the other by the misfortunes of war. Whole countrysides fled from the advance of the enemy, and large bags of prisoners were transferred to distant camps or shipped overseas. The institution of the Passover also involves a great migration. On the night when the Passover was eaten, more than two million people, whom we call the Children of Israel, left the land of Egypt for a new home. That was not caused by war, but by the direct hand of God, who planned great things for His people.

We might call it the birth of a nation, for it was that night that the people, who were slaves for generations, were molded into a nation, united under leadership which was God-given. Our American nation was born on the fourth of July, 1776, and we celebrate that event every year. Thus, too, the Israelites celebrated their deliverance by the hand of God by gathering their families together and eating the Passover lamb. The celebration of the Passover was one of the chief Jewish festivals, but its great importance lay not so much in the memories that it called to mind as in the blessings that it prefigured. The lamb that was killed and eaten every year by Jewish families is one of the types of Christ which speak eloquently of the Passion and death of our Lord.

Of all the types of Christ that we have in the Old Testament, the Passover lamb is the most beautiful and impressive. The facts which preceded the institution of the Passover are very interesting indeed. For several hundred years Israel had been in Egypt, ever since Joseph had brought his father and his family to that land. For a long time they were treated kindly, but then there was a change of dynasty, and that meant a change in the policy of government. They were oppressed and became virtual slaves and were treated unmercifully, but the Lord was watching in the heavens, as He always does, and when the time came, He prepared an escape for them. He called Moses and sent him to the king demanding the release of His people.

But mere words made little impression upon the king. So God sent a series of plagues, and every plague was preceded by the command: "Let My people go that they may serve Me." Pharoah is one of the many persons portrayed in the Bible that brought about their own destruction because of disobedience. You see what God demands is obedience. That is what He asks of you and me, that we surrender ourselves to Him. That He asked of the Lord Jesus, as we can see in the Garden of Gethsemane when Jesus submitted to His Father's plans and said: "Not My will, but Thine be done." But the one thing that God wanted was the one thing that Pharoah did not do. And so the plagues became worse, and Pharoah was frightened. While he was afraid, he always made promises to obey, but the promises were only superficial, and when the danger was over, he forgot about them.

During the war we heard much of foxhole religion, but the chaplains who returned to our country told us that the kind of religion which existed only in the foxholes was not worth very much. To be sure, God wants us to call upon Him whenever we are in trouble, but God wants our hearts not only when we are in need or when we are terrified. God wants our love and devotion and worship at all times.

Finally the patience of God was exhausted, and the tenth and last plague was brought upon the obstinate king and his people. It was the spring of the year, and night had fallen. Terror descended upon that country. The Lord passed over it and killed the first-born. But before He executed this judgment upon the Egyptians, Israel was directed to take a lamb, one year old and without blemish, to kill it, roast it, to gather the family together, and to eat it in the evening with unleavened bread and bitter herbs. The blood was to be sprinkled upon the lintel and on the posts of the door. That was God's saving mark. Whenever the Lord saw the blood, He passed over without bringing death to that family. Thus it happened that while there was not an Egyptian house that was spared, from the king's palace to the pauper's hut, in the homes of the Hebrews there was peace and security because there was blood on the doors. That very night two million people left Egypt. Such is the historic event which was commemorated every year as a reminder of the bitter experiences these people had and of their glorious deliverance.

But it had an added and richer significance. It was designed to prefigure an event which God had planned from eternity, namely, the salvation of the world. For the Passover celebration is a beautiful and impressive type of Christ and of His redemption. And again, as in the case of the offering of Isaac and of Joseph and his brethren, it is quite surprising how many parallels there are. That is true not only of the Passover lamb itself, but also of the circumstances that surrounded it. The Israelites were in slavery. They were freed by the power of God. So man was freed from sin. Christ died to make men free. The Israelites were saved from death. So Christ saved us from death and brought life and immortality to light. The Israelites were under hard taskmasters. So Satan is a hard taskmaster, who delights in sin, misery, and destruction. But when Christ said: "It is finished," the battle was over, and the victory had been won. Thus the great deliverance of the Israelites prefigured the truth of the Second Article that Christ has redeemed me from sin, from death, and from the power of the devil.

In like manner the Passover lamb is a type of Christ. It was without blemish. It was to be not more than one year old, that is, in the prime of life. It was to be roasted with fire, not a bone was to be broken. In like manner the fire of God's wrath descended upon the holy, innocent Son of God. Especially is the blood significant, for Christ shed His blood to save us from death. Thus the Passover lamb prefigured Him, of whom the Baptist said: "Behold the Lamb of God, which taketh away the sin of the world." That last note is the theme that runs through the entire Bible from beginning to end, salvation through the blood of Christ. That is the foundation on which the Children of God at all times have based their hope of heaven.

Now, as we think of the saving blood of the lamb, which prefigured the saving blood of Christ, there comes to our mind a dramatic incident in the Passion story. Jesus was before the Roman governor. Pilate knew that Jesus was innocent, and yet he sends Him to the Cross. But he feels the need of saving his face and calls for a basin of water, indicating thereby that he is washing his hands of the whole matter. Of course he committed a grievous wrong, but Pilate's act gives rise to the howl of the furious mob. A thousand voices cry: "His blood be on us and on our children!" If perhaps we feel some pity when we think of Pilate, we cannot feel anything but horror at the cry of the mob. Little did they know what the words implied. Little did they know how terribly it was to be fulfilled forty years later, when their city was destroyed and many thousands of its people met a cruel death. That put an end to their national life, and ever since they have been a homeless people. Not even today can they find peace in the land of their fathers. Go to Jerusalem and see them at the Wailing Wall. It is a touching and pitiable sight, these old men and women with tears running down their cheeks, thumbing their prayer books and kissing the stones that once were part of the wall enclosing the Temple area. The Jews are a people remarkably gifted. The world owes them a great debt, and yet there seems to be a shadow resting upon them.

Of course, that is no justification of the cruelties and

persecutions they have been made to suffer throughout the centuries. But this is a fact that ought to be recorded that where there is a persistent refusal to accept Christ, the result will always be tragedy. God is patient and long-suffering. He does not desire the death of the sinner, but when men do not turn to Christ for forgiveness, God must eventually say: "Depart from Me."

Moreover, we must not forget that there are many others besides the children of Abraham who call the curse of God down upon themselves. When men lead ungodly lives, when they injure and kill, steal and defraud, when they give themselves to immorality, what are they doing but hurrying Christ to the Cross? When people harden their hearts to God's gracious appeal, when they deaden their conscience, when they refuse to join Christians in their worship, they are choosing their eternal doom as surely as did Pharoah when he refused to be obedient to the command of God or as surely as those who cried before Pilate: "His blood be on us and on our children!"

That was a dreadful cry uttered by the mob on that fateful day, but like other expressions in the Passion story this one, too, may have a beautiful and wonderful meaning if we take it in another sense. Let us make this a personal matter and admit that the blood of Christ is upon us also. We, too, are guilty of His death, for He was "wounded for our transgressions and was bruised for our iniquities." But it is also true that by that very blood we are redeemed and made the children of God. Blessed is the man who believes that the blood of Calvary was spilled not only by him, but for him. It is my prayer that this may always be your song of triumph and mine, that Christ has redeemed us "not with gold or silver, but with His holy precious blood and with His innocent suffering and death, that we may be His own and live under Him in His kingdom and serve Him in everlasting righteousness, innocence, and blessedness." Amen.

The Bread from Heaven

And when the dew that lay was gone up, behold, upon the face of the wilderness there lay a small round thing, as small as the hoarfrost on the ground. And when the Children of Israel saw it, they said one to another: It is manna; for they wist not what it was. And Moses said unto them: This is the bread which the Lord hath given you to eat.—EXODUS 16:14-15.

THE giving of manna in the wilderness belongs to the realm of the supernatural. It is one of the miracles God performed to nourish his people as they traveled from the land of slavery to the land of promise. It is more. It is one of the beautiful types of Christ in the Old Testament. Our Lord indicates that Himself when He says in John 6: "I am the living Bread, which came down from heaven. If any man eat of this Bread, he shall live forever." That is the reason why we want to think of it tonight at this Lenten service.

When the Israelites left Egypt and crossed the Red Sea, they began the march through the desert land which separates Egypt from Palestine. But we must not think of that country in the ordinary sense we attach to the word "desert" as a sandy waste. In that part of Arabia sand is rather the exception than the rule. We must think of it as a wild country with rocks and mountains, with an occasional green fruitful valley from which the tribes that roam around there get their supplies.

Here, however, was a people of more than two million souls, and they had not been in this country many days when the question of food became a very pressing one. For the supplies brought along from Egypt were soon exhausted. But God, who led them out and planned their future, was watching over them. One morning they found the ground everywhere covered with a substance that was made up of small white kernels. The people did not know what it was, and so they said "man-hu," the Hebrew for "What is it?" Moses told them that it was the bread God sent from heaven. Every man was to gather an omer, which is about three quarts, every day and on Friday double the amount. The remarkable thing was that it was new every morning. For forty years this manna fed God's people. It was clearly a miraculous, supernatural feeding. It cannot be explained in any other way. Thus God was watching over His people and satisfied their hunger.

Now, hunger, physical hunger, is usually a good sign. Hunger is a symptom of normal vigorous life, and a loss of appetite is often a symptom that something is wrong. But, on the other hand, what a calamity it is when there is hunger and it cannot be satisfied! What a pitiful situation when there is famine and people starve! It has been a bad winter for many people in Europe and Asia. Even the American people have never been so food-conscious as they are at present. Housewives everywhere are wrestling with the problem of how they can obtain the foods their families are accustomed to. Yet how fortunate are we in America in comparison with the starving millions in Europe and Asia! How blessed are we in our country, where we have enough to eat, and it is with a great deal of fervor that we ought to thank God at every meal for our daily bread. Moreover, the serious question before our American people is not: Where shall we get food in abundance? but: Will we open our hearts and hands so that the starving millions of the world may satisfy their hunger? May God help us to be compassionate and generous.

Now, everything that has been said about physical hunger is true also of the hunger of the soul, and it is interesting to know that some of the most beautiful passages in the Bible use imagery connected with food and drink. "As the heart panteth after the water brooks, so panteth my soul after Thee, O God," says the writer of a well-known Psalm. "Thou preparest a table before me in the presence of mine enemies," are the words of David in his immortal poem. "Blessed are they that hunger and thirst after righteousness," said Jesus in the Beatitudes. From all this it is perfectly clear that it is absolutely essential to a healthy Christianity to have the right kind of spiritual appetite. For bodily food will never feed the soul, neither will any other earthly thing to which men's hearts are attached.

On the other hand, it is a sign of spiritual health when a man desires food for his soul. The jailer of Philippi was on the road to recovery when he asked: "What must I do to be saved?" The publican in the Temple knew what his soul was craving when he said: "God be merciful to me, a sinner." How deep was the insight of the malefactor on the cross when he said: "Lord, remember me when Thou comest into Thy kingdom." Therefore it would be well if each of us would ask himself tonight: What is the deepest desire of my heart? Am I putting first things first? Am I giving my soul the food that it needs?

Now, what this spiritual food is may be seen from our Lord's reference to manna when He said: "I am the living

Bread come down from heaven." Here again we find, as in the previous types, that it is quite surprising how many points of comparison there are between manna and the Lord, who alone is able to give food to hungry souls. Manna came from God, from heaven, and so did Christ. Israel was not able to feed itself. So man cannot save himself.

There was no substitute for manna. The Israelites either had to eat it or starve. So there is no substitute for the Gospel of Christ. As we say that, we hear our Lord declare: "I am the Way, the Truth, and the Life. No man cometh unto the Father but by Me." Manna supplied food to all alike, to the leaders as well as to the common people, to men, women, and children. As God looks upon humanity, He sees that men are all alike, "for all have sinned and come short of the glory of God." It matters not who we are, we all need the forgiveness which Christ obtained for us.

Manna supplied the wants of the children of Israel for forty years, day after day. So Christ is with us during the whole journey of life. He comes to us in Holy Baptism, in the instruction and guidance which we receive in the house of God, at the Communion table, where He gives us His body and blood, in adversity, in prosperity, and in the hour of death.

Particularly instructive is the question that people asked: "man-hu"? A similar question was asked when Jesus began His ministry. "Who is this Jesus of Nazareth?" When He returned to His home town the first time, His fellow townsmen were amazed. They thought they knew Him, but in reality they did not know Him at all. When He fed the five thousand, the amazement and enthusiasm was so great that they wanted to make Him king. When He was before Pilate, this Roman official marveled at Christ's dignity and majesty so that this Roman, to whom the life of another man meant nothing at all, tried his utmost to save Him. The centurion said of Him: "This was a righteous Man and the Son of God." That also is the verdict not only of these men, but of all history. He is the Wonder of the ages. There is no adequate explanation for that except the one from His own lips, "I am the living Bread come down from heaven."

We are reminded here especially of an incident that occurred toward the end of His ministry. It happened way up north, at the foot of Mount Hermon, where the Jordan has its source and is fed by the melting snows. There our Lord spent several days in seclusion with His disciples. There He had a heart-to-heart talk with them about a subject of great importance, for He knew that the end of His life was drawing near. He asked them what rightly has been called the Question of the Ages: "Whom do men say that I, the Son of Man, am?" There are many questions on which we can afford to suspend judgment or about which we can even be ignorant, but not this one, for upon the answer to this question depends our happiness for all time to come. For this question is an intensely personal one for all of us, as it was for the disciples. There, on the slope of Mount Hermon, as they looked down upon the city of Caesarea Philippi with its heathen temples and palaces, symbols of the glories of Greece and of Rome, Jesus asked His disciples: "But whom say ye that I am?" And the answer came back: "Thou art the Christ, the Son of the living God." That is the confession which the Christian Church has made ever since. That is what we say in the Creed: "I believe that Jesus Christ, true God, begotten of the Father from eternity, and also true Man, born of the Virgin Mary, is my Lord." I believe that because He is the Son of God and the Son of Man, He could die for me and triumph over sin and death.

In view of this, may I ask you: Are you taking advantage of the Lenten season? Are you drawing closer to Christ? Are you learning more of His love for you and of the meaning of His death on the Cross? Are you partaking more eagerly of this heavenly food? Let us not take the attitude of the Israelites in the wilderness. In later years they loathed this food from heaven. They grew tired of it. In like manner Christ was accepted and then rejected, with the crowd crying: "Crucify Him, crucify Him!" Rather, as hungry sheep let us always look up to Him to be fed. As God in the Arabian wilderness supplied the needs of the Israelites, and as Christ fed the five thousand, so God is eager now to supply all your wants. He knows what you need. He knows the secret longings of your soul, the wish to be a better Christian. He knows your anxieties and fears, the feeling of your own unworthiness. All these He sees and is eager to give to you according to your needs. So today He rejoices that you are here. He is happy whenever you come to His house and especially when you are a guest at His table, for here we receive the Bread of Life, the Bread broken for us on the Cross. He and He alone is able to supply all our wants. Amen.

The Rock in the Wilderness

And all the congregation of the Children of Israel journeyed from the wilderness of Sin, after their journeys, according to the commandment of the Lord, and pitched in Rephidim: and there was no water for the people to drink. And the people murmured against Moses and said, Wherefore is this that thou hast brought us up out of Egypt, to kill us and our children and our cattle with thirst? And Moses cried unto the Lord, saying: What shall I do unto this people? They be almost ready to stone me. And the Lord said unto Moses: Go on before the people and take with thee of the elders of Israel; and thy rod, wherewith thou smotest the river, take in thine hand, and go. Behold, I will stand before thee there upon the rock in Horeb; and thou shalt smite the rock, and there shall come water out of it, that the people may drink.—Exodus 17:1.3-6.

It is a sorely distressed people which this Word of God presents to us. A great number of men, women, and children are plodding along with drooping heads and parched bodies, for there isn't any water wherewith to quench their thirst. They are sick and faint and ready to die.

I remember the character of this territory very well. It is the northwest section of the Arabian Desert, the desolate country between Egypt and the Dead Sea, and there is still vivid in my memory a long day spent amid these forbidding hills and rocks. We had spent several fascinating days at Petra, the old home of the Edomites, and were ready to return to Jerusalem and civilization. We broke camp at night and began the northward march at the rising of the sun. With the help of a Bedouin guide we expected to reach a well by the middle of the afternoon, but the afternoon came, and there was no tree, shrub, or blade of grass in sight. We marched on after the setting of the sun for hours through the darkness, and it was not until ten o'clock at night that we came to a muddy pool of water. But while plodding along that hot afternoon and during the sultry hours of the night, hours after the last drop of water had disappeared from our canteens, we not only experienced thirst for ourselves, but thought also of how often the Bible uses physical thirst as an illustration of the deep desires of the believing soul for God, His help and His salvation. The writer of the Forty-Second Psalm says: "As the heart panteth after the water brooks, so panteth my soul after Thee, O God." And many times since has there come to me the word of the Lord Jesus: "I am the Water of Life."

It was through this desolate country that the Israelites were marching. It was there that they experienced the tortures of thirst, so much so that they wished themselves back in Egypt. Moses cried to Heaven for help and was heard. He was directed to take a rod and strike a great rock, and immediately it was cleft, and out gushed a stream of water. That was an evidence of the goodness of God. It was a proof of the fact that God always cares for His people, that He never sends us out upon any task without giving us the means and the strength to carry on.

But the rock in the wilderness means more than that. For its deeper meaning we turn to the New Testament. There we find Paul writing in First Corinthians 10 and referring to the miracle that happened to the Israelites: "Our fathers did all drink the same spiritual drink, for they drank of that spiritual Rock, and that Rock was Christ." Christ is the Rock of Ages, cleft for us. Therefore in this rock in the wilderness which furnished water to the thirsting Israelites we have a beautiful Old Testament type of Christ and of His salvation, just as thirst of the body is a picture of thirst of the soul.

We all know that it is essential for this life that the wants of the body are satisfied. We need food and drink and cannot live without them. We saw that last Wednesday when we heard of manna, the bread from heaven. But though food and drink are essential, that is not enough. "Man cannot live by bread alone," Jesus said in the wilderness; and: "Whosoever drinketh this water will thirst again," he said to the Samaritan woman at Jacob's well. Our hunger and thirst are very real, but we share them with the creatures of a lower order. An animal needs food and drink as much as we do, and if it will not get food and drink, it will starve and die. But beyond that there is not much that an animal needs or wants. Its world is small and circumscribed. But we human beings have a higher thirst, for we are made not only as the animals, from the dust of the ground, but the Spirit of God was breathed into us when we were created. We were given an immortal soul. That means that man has a thirst not only for beauty, culture, learning, progress, for human fellowship, for joint enterprise, but, above all, for peace with God. Our greatest longing is not for food and drink and money and the things that money can buy, not even for culture and beauty and learning, but for God, who is merciful and forgiving and does not forsake us in the day of trouble or in the hour of death.

Now, it was just to give us such a God that Christ came to earth and went the way of sorrows. Thus from the rock in the wilderness we come to Calvary. As we stand again at the foot of the Cross, there is one word from His dying lips that appeals to us tonight and is especially significant. It is the shortest of His seven words, "I thirst." Seven times the Savior spoke, but only twice did He express the agony that He suffered. He prayed for forgiveness for His enemies. He opened Paradise for the dying malefactor, He made provision for His bereaved mother, and at the close of His agony there is the cry of victory, "It is finished," and finally He commended His soul into the hands of His heavenly Father. But there are two words that express great agony of body and of soul. When darkness settled down upon Him and He was overwhelmed by hell, He cried: "My God, My God, why hast Thou forsaken Me?" and soon after that: "I thirst."

That shows that His sufferings were real and that both in body and soul Christ is our Substitute. Christ died for us that our sins might be taken away, that it again may be possible for us to come into the presence of a merciful God. His thirst is part of His redemptive work. What He suffered on the Cross He suffered for us so that we might not sink down into the realm of everlasting thirst, so that we might be numbered among those about the throne of God of whom we read in the Revelation of Saint John: "They shall hunger no more neither thirst any more, for the Lamb, which is in the midst of the throne, shall feed them and shall lead them to living fountains of water." Thus Christ is the Rock in the wilderness of this world, because from Him issue streams of living water.

Then there is another thing that we can learn when we put side by side the thirst of the Israelites and the thirst of Jesus. When the children of Israel thirsted in the wilderness, they showed that they were thoroughly human. They had their human needs and distresses. When Christ cried: "I thirst," He also showed that His humanity was real and genuine. He was flesh of my flesh and blood of my blood. He had the same bodily needs that I have. He experienced what we so often experience, hunger and thirst, pain and sorrow. Because He, too, is human and lived here in this vale of tears, He knows all my frailties and weaknesses. He looks upon me with infinite compassion and reaches out His hand to support me. Whenever I have to face the burdens and sorrows of life, even when I walk through the valley of the shadow of death, I am not alone. I need fear no evil, for He is with me and understands my needs and is eager to supply my wants.

Even the consciousness of my guilt cannot rob me of the blessed assurance of His presence and compassion, and especially when my sins rise up against me, I am able confidently to pray,

Rock of Ages, cleft for me,
  Let me hide myself in Thee;
Let the water and the blood
  From Thy riven side which flowed
Be of sin the double cure,
  Cleanse me from its guilt and power.

As we leave the rock in the wilderness, there comes to mind another poem, the first verse of which, perhaps, you all know.

Beneath the Cross of Jesus
  I fain would take my stand,
The shadow of a mighty rock
  Within a weary land;
A home within the wilderness,
  A rest upon the way
From the burning of the noontide heat
  And the burden of the day.

Christ, the Rock in the wilderness! What a Rock it is! My Life, my Refuge, and my Strength! Amen.

The Brazen Serpent

And they journeyed from Mount Hor by the way of the Red Sea to compass the land of Edom; and the soul of the people was much discouraged because of the way. And the people spake against God and against Moses: Wherefore have ye brought us up out of Egypt to die in the wilderness? For there is no bread, neither is there any water; and our soul loatheth this light bread. And the Lord sent fiery serpents among the people, and they bit the people; and much people of Israel died. Therefore the people came to Moses and said: We have sinned, for we have spoken against the Lord and against thee; pray unto the Lord that He take away the serpents from us. And Moses prayed for the people. And the Lord said unto Moses: Make thee a fiery serpent, and set it upon a pole; and it shall come to pass that everyone that is bitten, when he looketh upon it, shall live. And Moses made a serpent of brass and put it upon a pole, and it came to pass, that if a serpent had bitten any man, when he beheld the serpent of brass, he lived.—NUMBERS 21:4-9.

AGAIN we are in spirit with the children of Israel in the wilderness. The last two Wednesday evenings we also traveled with them as they were on the way to the Promised Land, and at both occasions we saw evidence of the bountiful goodness of God. When there was nothing to eat, He sent bread from heaven. When they had no water to quench their thirst, He opened the rock in the wilderness. But we found not only that these gifts of bread and water were an evidence of the goodness of God, they were also beautiful Old Testament types of Christ.

Today, again, we see this great multitude of men, women, and children plodding along. But now they are not only tired and faint, they are ungrateful, sullen, and rebellious. For almost forty years they have been in the wilderness, and they were tired of marching about year after year without apparently getting any nearer to the occupation of the land that had been promised to them. So they rebelled against God for not making good the promise He had given them long ago. They rebelled against Moses for leading them on what they believed to be a hopeless enterprise. Once more they wished themselves back in Egypt and even expressed their disgust at being obliged to eat the manna which God had given them from heaven. So there was nothing left for God to do but to punish the disobedient and rebellious people. We are told that He sent fiery serpents among them. That is, they were attacked by venomous snakes whose bites produced violent inflammation and death. Of course it was not long before they realized how grievously they had sinned, and then they implored God through Moses to forgive them and help them. Again their great intercessor prayed, and the prayer was heard. God commanded Moses to make a serpent of brass and to put it upon a pole, promising that everyone who would look upon the serpent in faith would be healed. The result was immediate. Peace was once more established, and they continued on their way. This certainly shows the forgiving love of God.

But it means more. For a deeper meaning we again turn to the New Testament. There we hear our Lord Himself say to Nicodemus: "As Moses lifted up the serpent in the wilderness, even so must the Son of Man be lifted up, that whosoever believeth in Him should not perish, but have eternal life." Christ raised on the Cross is the One to whom we look for healing of our souls. Therefore, in the serpent in the wilderness we have another impressive Old Testament type of Christ, of His Passion and His salvation, just as in the sin of the children of Israel we have a picture of our own transgressions and of the penalties they bring.

Perhaps we are guilty of sins very much like those committed by the Israelites in the wilderness. Isn't it true that we sometimes demand that God should shape things to suit and please ourselves, and if He does not do so immediately, we become dissatisfied, sullen, and rebellious and forget the many times He answered our prayers? Is it not true that, as Israel desired to go back to Egypt and into slavery, so there is a continual struggle within us to yield to temptation? As Israel was disgusted with the manna, we too lose taste for the Word of God, for the services in His house, and for the Sacrament. Is it not true that we in our souls and bodies bear the wounds of the old serpent, the great enemy of man? Like the Israelites, we have been bitten, and the bite is fatal. For "the wages of sin is death." But it is also true that God is willing to forgive and to receive us again.

As we think of the brazen serpent and its purpose, let us note two other points of comparison. Moses was not directed to place a real serpent upon a pole, but one of brass. It looked like a serpent, but it was without poison. Thus Christ had our human nature, but was without sin. Let us also note that the serpent was not made of silver and gold, which are used chiefly for ornamentation, but of brass, which is a common, useful metal. So Christ laid aside His majesty and left the golden throne of heaven and humiliated Himself to the Cross; but thereby He became infinitely useful so that "whosoever believeth in Him should not perish, but have everlasting life." We see, then, as we travel with the children of Israel in the wilderness that we are brought face-to-face with the uplifted Cross. The brazen serpent is a symbol. It is a symbol of the forgiveness of God. So the Cross is a symbol, the symbol of the sacrifice that our Lord made for us. Thus from the wilderness we again come to Calvary. As we stand there at the foot of the Cross, conscious of a great deal of confusion and noise, there comes out of that babel of noise one word of his enemies more important than any other: "He saved others, Himself He cannot save." That was one of the hateful, taunting remarks that they cast into His teeth, and yet there is a remarkable truth in those words. They not merely show unspeakable hatred and pitiless cruelty, but contain a blessed Gospel truth. Especially are these words a commentary on the "must" that Jesus used when He spoke to Nicodemus, "As Moses lifted up the serpent in the wilderness, so must the Son of Man be lifted up." If the world is to be saved, that can be done only through a great sacrifice, and the Son of God is the only one that can make that sacrifice.

It is a well-known fact that sacrifice is a part of human experience. Sometimes it is necessary that some lives be sacrificed in order that others might be saved. As when a man saves someone from drowning or from death in a fire and thereby loses his own life; or when a missionary gives his life out of love for lost souls. It is just that which applies to Jesus, though in an infinitely higher and nobler sense. For there was only one way to save a sinning and dying world. If the sins of the world were to be atoned for, God Himself had to give His life. He had to give Himself into the hands of His enemies and be lifted to the Cross. Because Jesus paid the great price, you can now look up to God and say: "Father," and the Father can look at you and say: "My son, my daughter, be of good cheer, thy sins are forgiven thee." That is the message which is designed to bring you the peace of heaven and make you God's happy child. Thus the Cross is not only a symbol of sacrifice, it is also a symbol of healing and forgiveness.

There is an old legend that Saint Helena, the mother of Emperor Constantine, made it the object of her life to find the Cross of Christ. As her workmen were digging at the traditional Mount Calvary in Jerusalem, they found three crosses, but which one of these three was Christ's Cross? To test out the crosses, the workmen brought one to a very ill person in the city, and upon the sight of that cross the person became worse. They brought the second cross, and the patient became a raving maniac. These were the crosses apparently of the two malefactors. But when the workmen brought the third cross, the person so desperately ill became calm and was immediately healed of his illness. Thus the identity of the true cross was established. We know this is only a legend and has in it the unchristian element of magic so prominent in *The Robe,* a best seller of a few years back. But the legend does bring to our mind an all-important truth. It is at the Cross of Christ, and only there, that we can find forgiveness and peace. It is only there that we can find victory over sin, sorrow, pain, and death. Thus also the serpent in the wilderness represents the sum and substance of the Christian religion, which Paul put into these words: "The wages of sin is death, but the gift of God is eternal life through our Lord Jesus Christ."

The final observation that we can make is this, that the brazen serpent was raised high above the camp, drawing people from everywhere, that they might receive health and healing. We are reminded here of the words of Jesus: "If I be lifted up, I will draw all men unto Myself." That is the drawing power of the Cross. It is a great magnet. At first He drew to Himself the Twelve. At the close of His ministry there were five hundred. On the day of Pentecost there were three thousand, and then they began to come from the far corners of the earth. The Christian centuries have proved that He is able to draw all men to Himself, and you, I trust, all of you, are among those who have been drawn to Him who loved you and gave Himself for you.

Tonight, again, we want to realize His love that knows no bounds. The serpent in the wilderness met a great need. Thus we find Christ to be the answer to all of our questions, for there is no need that His love cannot adequately meet. Perhaps you are ill and worried. You have made it a matter of fervent prayer, but apparently your prayer has not yet been heard. Do not be troubled, for Jesus desires your happiness and will help you in your need. Perhaps you are anxious about a son or a husband far away from home. You haven't heard from him for weeks. Is he still safe? But don't be anxious, for Jesus says to you and to him: "Lo, I am with you alway, even unto the end of the world." Whatever else it may be that is distressing you, place it into the hands of your Friend. And it is my prayer that no one will leave this house of God tonight without the assurance that the Lord Jesus is ready to give you whatever you need for your peace and happiness. Why can I give you this promise? What is the basis of my hope? Here it is. That He was lifted to the Cross. "For greater love hath no man than this, that he lay down his life for his friends." And our response will be that of the poet: "My faith looks up to Thee, Thou Lamb of Calvary, Savior divine." Amen.

The Table of the Lord

(MAUNDY THURSDAY)

Thou preparest a table before me in the presence of mine enemies.—PSALM 23:5.

EVEN if I had not indicated in the reading of the text that this verse is a part of the Twenty-Third Psalm, you would have known where to find it, for we are all familiar with this immortal poem, and many of us could recite it from memory. It has become a part of the poetic treasury of God's people and has meant infinitely much in comfort, strength, and inspiration to the children of God everywhere.

It is usually called the Shepherd Psalm, and we can readily see why, for it speaks of the shepherd, the pasture, the water, the protection by day and night. But when we call it the Shepherd Psalm, we have not exhausted its contents, for, and this may not be known to some, the imagery of the shepherd is not carried through the entire Psalm. Only the first four verses tell us about the shepherd and the care of his sheep. In verse five the imagery changes completely. "Thou preparest a table before me in the presence of mine enemies. Thou annointest my head with oil, my cup runneth over." We are not in the open country any more. The scene of pasture, brook, and valley where death is lurking give way to the picture of a palace where a great Lord has prepared a banquet for me, has anointed me, and prepared a table laden with delicious food, and my cup overflows with the choicest wine. While I am at the banquet table, the enemies who sought my life are outside, helplessly looking in. "Thou preparest a table before me in the presence of mine enemies." I am safe in the palace. I am enjoying the protection and generosity of my Lord.

Now, is this not a beautiful picture of the bountiful goodness of God? It is He who provides all things that His children need. It is He who has given us our life. It is He who has filled the earth with beauty, growth, and rich supplies; and when we pray: "Give us this day our daily bread," we confess that everything that supports our body and life comes from above. But it is also in another and deeper sense that God has prepared a banquet for us. Do you remember the Parable of the Great Supper? It tells of the Lord who prepared a banquet and invited us. The reference there is not to the gifts of the body, but of the soul. The Great Supper is the great salvation God has prepared before the world. The Great Supper includes all that Christ has accomplished for us on the Cross and now offers to us in His Word. Whenever we sit down to read the Bible or attend a Christian service, God is preparing a table, a feast for our souls. He does so "in the presence of mine enemies." I am sitting at the table of the Lord, and my enemies and all that are seeking my harm and destruction are helpless and powerless, for I am in the safekeeping of Almighty God.

Who are these enemies? We turn to the beautiful words of the explanation of the Second Article in Luther's Catechism. Christ has "redeemed me, a lost and condemned creature, purchased and won me from all sin, from death and from the power of the devil." I am at the table of the Lord, and sin can no longer give me a troubled conscience, neither am I afraid of death. In fact, I need have no worry whatsoever, either for myself or for my loved ones. For Jesus says to me: "Whatsoever ye shall ask the Father in My name, He will give it you." He will give me forgiveness, peace of mind, a sense of security, and the knowledge that all is well.

But the question I should now like to ask is this: Is that the firm belief of all of us, and do we live accordingly? Do we all say, My greatest wish is to sit at the table of the Lord and partake of its spiritual food? Or do some of us have to confess that we do love to sit at the table of the world? For there is always the danger that we feast on the material things men strive for. If so, let us resolve tonight to turn away from the things that satisfy a little while and return to the heavenly treasures that God so bountifully gives.

Now let us go a step farther in the contemplation of this text. Whatever is true of the Word of God as a feast of the soul, is especially true of the Sacrament of our Lord instituted on the night in which He was betrayed. It is that event that we are thinking of especially tonight. It was on the Thursday of the first Holy Week that the Lord Jesus gathered His disciples together to celebrate the Passover. He prepared a table in a physical sense for His disciples in the Upper Room. There was a lamb, bread, wine, and bitter herbs. Many, many years before God had saved His people from bondage, and in order that they should never forget it, they were to celebrate the Passover every year. But the Passover was to be celebrated for another reason also. To the believing children of God in the Old Testament it was to be not only a memorial of a great rescue by their Covenant God and a reminder of His constant presence, interest, and help, but also a celebration that pointed to greater future blessings. The Passover lamb, slain every year, had a deep significance in God's plan of redemption. Christ is "the Lamb of God that taketh away the sin of the world," "the Lamb slain from the foundation of the world." Accordingly, our Lord, with His disciples in the Upper Room, is not only celebrating the Passover, but giving them something new and far better.

A new period in the history of God's people was to begin. His suffering and death marked the end of the old. Now comes the new. So He instituted a feast to be celebrated as long as the Christian Church is upon the earth. We call this the Lord's Supper, and it made such a deep impression upon the disciples that we have four records of it. We think of it as the most precious possession that we have. Before Christ ascended into heaven, He said: "Lo, I am with you alway, even unto the end of the world." We know that He is with us in His Word, with His love, His help, His guidance; but especially is He with us in the Lord's Supper with His body and blood. "Thou preparest a table before me," so said David, and that is true in the highest sense in the Lord's Supper.

Jesus is in the shadow of the Cross. Soon His head will be crowned with thorns and His hands outstretched. But really He is not thinking of Himself, but of His disciples. He wants to strengthen and comfort them and give them the assurance of His love. They are in a world which at times may be hostile to them, and at other times may strongly appeal to them. That is true not only of the Twelve, not only of the early Christians, it is true throughout the centuries. He saw the need of your soul, your spiritual trials and temptations. He saw all your weaknesses and sins and wanted to assure you of His love, mercy, and redemption. That is why He prepared His table. He gives bread and wine, and as He does so, He gives you His precious body and blood. That is what we call the Lord's Table, Holy Communion. Do not ask me to explain the Real Presence. It goes beyond our understanding. But, thank

God, we do not have to understand it in order to receive its blessings. Just believe that what your Savior says to you is true, and rejoice.

It is here where we ought to note the intensely personal character of the entire Psalm. How prominent are the personal pronouns *I, my,* and *me.* Just read the Psalm to yourself, and emphasize these little but significant words, and see how precious they will become to you. "The Lord is *my* shepherd. *I* shall not want. He maketh *me* to lie down in green pastures. He leadeth *me* besides the still waters." That is true also of the verse before us today. "Thou preparest a table before *me* in the presence of *mine* enemies." It is you, and you, for whom the Lord is preparing His table, and this personal way in which God deals with His children is also one of the precious features of the Lord's Supper.

Everywhere in the Scriptures we are told of the love of God, of His willingness to forgive penitent sinners, of His eagerness to do everything for our happiness; and we have every right to believe all these promises. But in the Lord's Supper He does something more than merely address His children together. For as you come to His table, He comes to everyone of you separately, calling you by name, as it were, assuring you that His promises and His love are meant for you personally. As you receive the bread and wine, He gives to you, and to you, and to you, His body and His blood as a token that all this is eternally true for *you* and that *you* are His beloved child.

Of course, to receive the benefit of it all, we must feel our need and sinfulness. We must hunger and thirst for forgiveness and the love of God. If you truly confess: "God, be merciful unto me, a sinner!" if you believe that Christ died for you, then all that Christ has promised is yours.

And all of us, whether we are His guests or not, may leave the house of God with the conviction that it is a blessed thing to be a Christian, a believer in the Lord Jesus Christ, for in the presence of the Lord we always have security, joy, and peace. Amen.

The Bearer of Our Sins

(GOOD FRIDAY)

He is despised and rejected of men, a Man of Sorrows, and acquainted with grief; and we hid as it were our faces from Him; He was despised, and we esteemed Him not. Surely He hath borne our griefs and carried our sorrows; yet we did esteem Him stricken, smitten of God, and afflicted. But He was wounded for our transgressions, He was bruised for our iniquities; the chastisement of our peace was upon Him; and with His stripes we are healed.—ISAIAH 53:3-5.

THIS is the story of Good Friday. It is the story of the rejection, suffering, and death of the Son of God. It is the story of the Man of Sorrows, who took the sinners' place. It is a vivid account, and yet not written by an eyewitness nor by someone who received information from those who stood at the foot of the Cross. No, these words so beautiful and impressive were written hundreds of years before the Lord Jesus went upon the path that led to shame and death, for it is one of the sublime prophecies of the Old Testament.

The Old Testament is full of Christ. There are a great many incidents, facts, and objects in the ancient record which have a direct reference to Christ's life, work, and Passion. We had occasion to learn that, when at the Lenten services we heard how Abraham was ready to sacrifice Isaac, how Joseph forgave his brethren, how the Passover lamb was eaten, how God gave to His people bread from heaven and water from the rock, and how Moses erected the brazen serpent in the wilderness. But tonight we come to the climax of all Old Testament references to Christ as we hear the voice of the Prophet Isaiah, the greatest preacher of the Gospel before the days of the Son of Man. For even though Isaiah lived 700 years before the Christian era, he gives us a marvelous picture of the coming Redeemer. We can think of these different incidents in the Old Testament as hills from which we view Calvary. But the highest hill of vision in the Old Testament is the Fifty-Third Chapter of Isaiah. Given a vision such as no other man before him had, this great Old Testament Prophet foresees in the distance the Cross rising like a torch and shedding its light over the world darkened by sin. It is this that makes Isaiah the greatest Gospel preacher of the Old Testament, well worthy to speak to us on this day, which commemorates the death of Christ.

What does Isaiah see as he looks across the centuries? He sees a man forsaken and unspeakably lonely. He speaks of Him as "despised and rejected of men." That is true. When we view the Passion history, we are amazed at the noise and confusion everywhere, in the Garden of Gethsemane, in the court of the high priest, in the judgment hall of Pilate, and on Calvary. But in the midst of these places of confusion stands the figure of the lonely Christ. He is all alone. Never was anyone so lonely and forsaken. What shouting there had been a few days before when the people of Galilee, who were visiting Jerusalem, cried: "Blessed is He that cometh in the name of the Lord!" But on this day there was another cry from the people of that city: "Crucify Him!" He was forsaken by all those whom He had helped in their need, whom He had visited in their homes, whose loved ones He had raised from the dead, whose children He had blessed. Where were they now? He is indeed the lonely Christ. A still greater source of grief it was for Him to be forsaken by His own disciples. How He longed for their company in the Garden of Gethsemane! "Could ye not watch with Me one hour?" How it hurts one to hear that all disciples forsook Him and fled! One betrayed Him, another denied Him. The lonely Christ!

So today He is despised and rejected by the mocking world. Let us ponder this well. We do not want to follow in their footsteps. We do not want to join that black company. We want rather to watch with Him in His sorrow. Therefore I can assure you that He rejoices in what you are doing on this holy day. Even now, as He is seated at the right hand of God and looking down upon you and me gathered here to do Him honor, there is joy in heaven that you are giving Him your heart in this sacred hour. But the Lord does not want us to be close to Him only during this sacred season or when we are gathered with our fellow Christians in the house of God, but every day He wants our worship and our prayers. Moreover, He wants us to know that because He was lonely and rejected we never need to be lonely. "Lo, I am with you alway, even unto the end of the world."

What did Isaiah see? He saw Him who "was stricken, smitten of God, and afflicted." And that also is literally true, for we see an intense darkness settling down on Calvary. It was not the darkness of the night, for it was early in the afternoon. It was a horrifying and gruesome silence, broken only by the groans of agony of the malefactors and the mutterings of the multitude. Then through the horrible darkness comes the bitter cry: "My God, My God, why hast Thou forsaken Me?"

That is the climax of Christ's redemptive work. Then His soul suffered the tortures of hell. He was forsaken by His

Heavenly Father. There is nothing that happened on Calvary more strange, more deeply mysterious than this. A learned Christian scholar once told me that there are many things in the Christian religion which his infinite mind was not able to comprehend, but none was farther from his understanding than that the Father should forsake His Son. Of course we know what is implied and what it means for us even though we cannot grasp the inner fact. The sins of the world had risen like a wall and had hidden the Father's face. Upon Him were resting the sins of all men, the sins of the past, the sins of today, the sins of the ages to come, the sins that you and I commit so freely from day to day.

Yet Christ was the innocent Lamb of God. At a recent flower show in one of our Midwestern cities there was one flower that was given the highest award. It was a single blossom, a beautiful carnation of exceptional size and startling whiteness. When it was exhibited, it was shown against a background of black velvet. That is a picture of Calvary. A picture of the pure and holy Jesus over against the background of human sin. That also is so vividly portrayed by the fact that there are three crosses on Calvary. The central Cross always receives our greatest attention as it should, but the other two crosses are also deeply significant. The word "malefactor" in the Gospel story tells us what these two crosses stand for. These men were dying for their sins, for wrongs will ultimately always be crucified. Unrepented sins will always be punished. Just read your daily papers and see how dishonesty, immorality, wickedness of every kind, finally meets its cross upon which it is crucified.

This, then, gives us the divine significance of Calvary. Between the two malefactors dying for their sins is Christ, the Righteous. He is the innocent, the holy One, dying for the guilty. This great fact, too, must become deeply personal, and we can put the meaning of the Cross into four simple words: "Christ died for *me*." That, too, was part of the vision that Isaiah had: "Surely He hath borne *our* griefs and carried *our* sorrows. He was wounded for *our* transgressions, He was bruised for *our* iniquities. The chastisement of *our* peace was upon Him, and with His stripes *we* are healed."

Did you notice the *our* and the *we*? Not only were we *guilty* of what happened to Him on Calvary, it was for *us*, for *our* peace and happiness, that He endured it all. It was for *us* that His sweat, like great drops of blood, fell down upon the ground in Gethsemane. It was for *us* that He was shamefully treated as a common criminal before His human judges. It was for *us* that He was sacrificed on the altar of the Cross and that He endured the terrors of hell. When once we realize that, we will look at ourselves in an entirely new light. Not only will we never doubt the love of God and always believe in His forgiveness, but here, too, is the greatest incentive in the world to be like Him.

Have you experienced some great distress? He carried that sorrow to the Cross so that your burden would be light and your sorrow be turned into joy. Do you feel how far you have come short of what God expects of you? Have you become lukewarm in your prayers and your worship? He was wounded and bruised so that there would be a new love for God in your heart. Is it hard for you to forgive? Are your actions governed by envy, by ill will to others? Are you tempted to be unclean in thought and speech? He was stricken and smitten that every sin of yours would be wiped out and you be given the power to cast these things out of your life. He saw every need of your soul, all your spiritual trials and temptations. He saw your weaknesses and sins and asks you to repent, to be deeply sorry; and having brought you to repentance, He wants to assure you of His love and mercy. He wants you to know that you are forgiven and reconciled to God and now have the power to follow His example.

To assure you of this still more, He has given you the Lord's Supper. Therefore come with joy to the Sacrament, for it is advisedly that we speak of celebrating the Lord's Supper. It is indeed a celebration, an occasion of joy. To be sure, there ought to be a preparation when we kneel and confess our sins, but having done that, we come to the Lord's Table with a song in our hearts because of the renewed assurance we shall be given of God's mercy and grace.

But to all of you He gives the assurance of His love. He tells you that there is no need for which His love is not adequate. All of us, whether we are His guests today or not, may leave the house of God with the conviction that it is a blessed thing to be a child of God through Him who loved us and gave Himself for us. May He always give us peace and joy in believing. Amen.

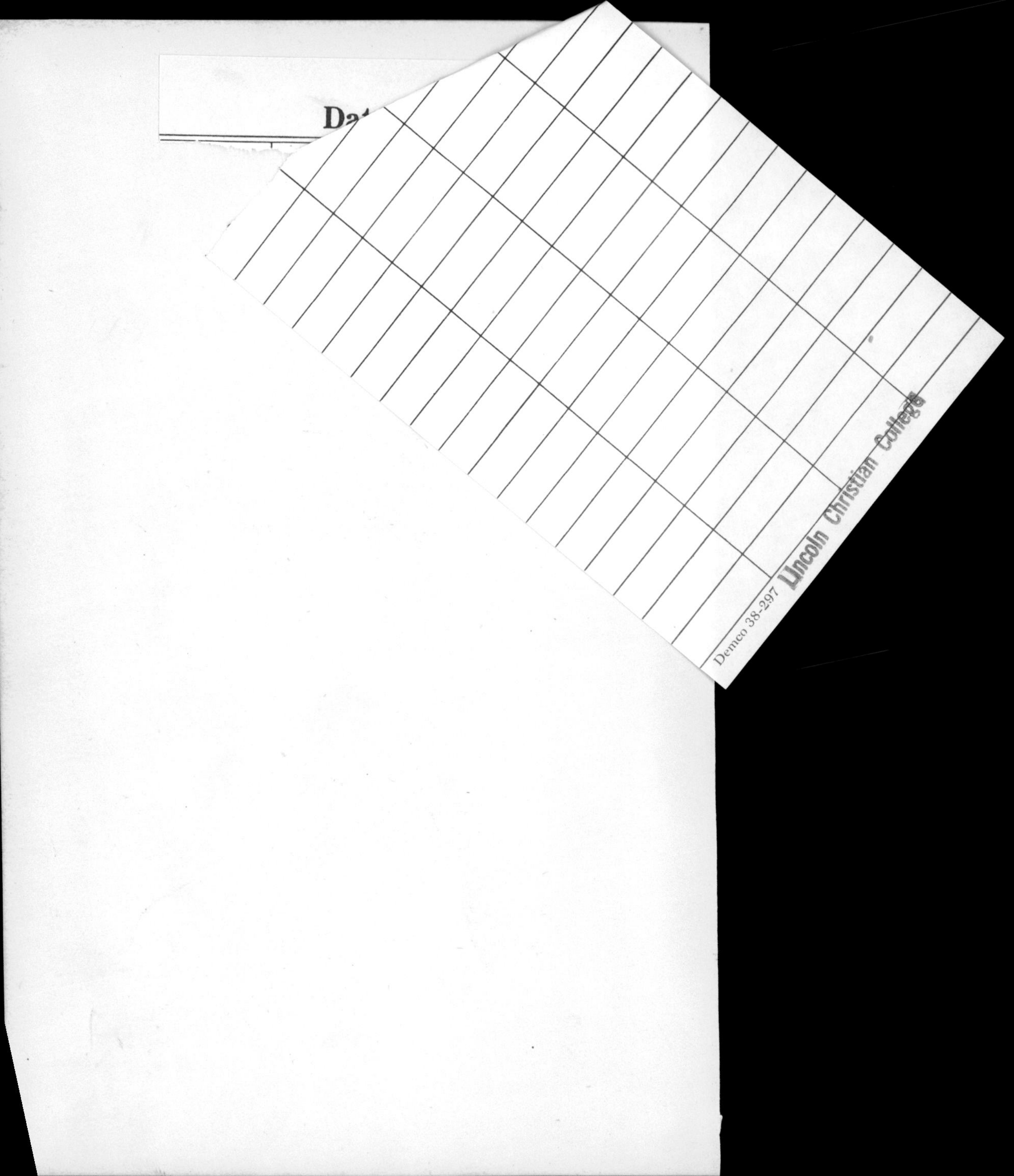
Dat
Demco 38-297
Lincoln Christian College